Maxene holds a Masters of Education in Adult Communication from the University of Toronto as well as a B.A. in English and minor in Education from the State University of New York. Her professional experience includes High school English Teacher, Manager of Human Resources and Senior Account Executive for several human resource consulting firms in both the United States and Canada. She and her husband, Lee, enjoy a close relationship with their blended family of two sons and two daughters as well as seven grandchildren. Maxene currently resides in Alpharetta, GA.

Dedication

To Richard and Sherley Raices, who did the best they could.

Maxene Raices

THE LAND OF SUNSHINE AND HELL

A Memoir of a 60's Unwed Mother

AUSTIN MACAULEY PUBLISHERS™

London • Cambridge • New York • Sharjah

Ordering Information:
Quantity sales: special discounts are available on quantity purchases by corporations, associations, and others. For details, contact the publisher at the address below.

Publisher's Cataloging in Publication data
Raices, Maxene
The Land Of Sunshine and Hell

ISBN 9781641822206 (Paperback)
ISBN 9781641822190 (Hardback)
ISBN 9781641822183 (E-Book)

The main category of the book—.Biography & Autobiography/ Women

www.austinmacauley.com/us

First Published (2018)
Austin Macauley Publishers ™ LLC
40 Wall Street, 28th Floor
New York, NY 10005
USA

mail-usa@austinmacauley.com
+1 (646) 5125767

Acknowledgment

This memoir has been percolating for fifty years, waiting to be born. The insights and support of several people made it possible for me to complete the project, including Elissa Hadley-Conklin, Brenda Sevcik, Mary Lou Mazzara, Betsy Scott, the Atlanta Writer's Club Writing Critique Group, Romolo Maurizi, and of course my patient, loving, supportive husband, Lee McGuire.

The stories in this book reflect the author's recollection of events. Some names, locations, and identifying characteristics have been changed to protect the privacy of those depicted. Dialog has been re-created from memory.

Prologue

My boyfriend, Romolo, and his parents arrived at my house after dinner, humbly shuffling into our living room, a room almost equal in size to their entire walk up apartment situated over a dusty antique store. They took their positions. Romolo collapsed into one of the chairs next to the fireplace. His mother, Nerina, nodded hello and cracked a crooked half smile at my parents, head bowed as she sat in the chair on the opposite side of the fireplace. His father, Giannino, and my father took their places on the dining room chairs that had been brought in to the living room. My mother and I sat on the couch opposite the fireplace. The tension in the room thickened the air. I was barely breathing. My mother spoke first.

"Thank you for coming over. We need to discuss what our options are for dealing with The Situation."

I was seventeen and pregnant. What were my options? Abortion was neither legal nor easily accessible in 1964. Romolo was nineteen and had just finished his first year of college. I was looking forward to starting college in the fall. We had dated for a year and were in love, naïve, and scared. How could this have happened? We had no clue about sex or that petting and 'making out' could lead to an unwanted pregnancy.

It was Sunday. The rain pinged on the roof like popcorn, then the sun suddenly peeked from behind the lavender tinged clouds, smiling with the promise of better times. It was as if the sky was crying and then cracking an occasional grin as the meeting got underway.

Chapter One
The Meeting, 1964

There was an awkward, heavy silence. I glanced at Nerina. She embodied unhappiness. Years of marital emptiness had etched lines down her face that told a story of sadness. Her black sweater was buttoned to the neck, just barely revealing a flower print blouse. A gold cross hung limply on a chain over her collar. The black skirt, dark stockings, and practical shoes gave the impression she could have been a nun in street clothes. She kept her eyes lowered, glancing occasionally at her son for direction. Looking at his mother, it was clear where Romolo had gotten some of his good looks. Warm, sad, brown eyes squinted at us, silently exhibiting the pain her lips did not express. Dark, wavy, brown hair was just beginning to grow streaks of gray, and was pulled neatly away from her face.

She hardly looked at me, spoke little English, and understood only enough to get by. If she understood what was being discussed, she nodded, all the while grimacing with half closed eyes, as if she was coping with a pain somewhere deep in her black swathed body. Hands lay in her lap; she fidgeted with a tissue. I thought to myself:

Had she been crying on her way to this meeting or was this just a sign of her frayed nerves?

Romolo sat slumped in his chair, eyes averted. He had declared his love for me many times over the last year, but now, faced with the reality of my pregnancy, he had nothing to say. He looked powerless, waiting for someone else to figure out a solution. Nerina was the first to speak.

"I take bambino. I good mama!"

A huge invisible band was tightening around my throat. My head screamed silently.

"No! I'm sorry, but that won't work!" I blurted out. "This child needs to be raised by an English-speaking parent." I couldn't imagine a baby being raised by this sad, depressed woman who barely spoke English. I heard myself speaking in a quiet monotone, not allowing my true emotion to show. I shook my head and realized she might need a translator to fully understand. My thoughts revealed my true concerns:

How could this option ever be a possibility? My child would be a stranger to me, speaking another language as its mother tongue. In fact, given Nerina's history, who can promise she won't take the baby back to Italy every time she feels she needs to see her doctors? No! This can't happen!

She wrinkled her brow as her son explained my comment. The knot in my stomach enlarged and my fingers laced into a rock on my lap. Romolo continued to sit silently deflated in his chair. His whole demeanor appeared to transform into a child, not a young man who was partly responsible for the situation. I felt like screaming at him.

How can you just sit there? Don't you have anything to say or any ideas? You told me you loved me, but now I feel abandoned and very unloved. Why do I feel so alone in this moment?

My mother volunteered Option Two. "Maybe I can raise the child until you finish college," she suggested in a low, tentative voice. "You could spend time with the baby when you come home at school breaks."

I recoiled at her suggestion. In my mind, it was half-hearted.

"Mom, c'mon. Be realistic. This is not what you want to spend your time doing at this stage of your life. Besides, knowing the baby is with you would distract me from even attempting to do my work at school! And how confusing it would be for the child to figure out who their mother is!"

My heart ached as I realized that Romolo would not step forward with any suggestion for us to be together with the baby. Only silence and brooding. I guess I should have been grateful that he showed up with his parents to officially 'own' the problem. Now that he was in my living room, I still felt abandoned.

We sat in a circle of deafening quiet. I looked at Romolo who continued to sit slumped in his chair as if he had been called to the principal's office for misbehaving. He couldn't even look at me. His arms crossed defensively as he squirmed, looking down at the floor. He looked totally uncomfortable. He had contributed to the situation, and now he hoped someone else would solve the problem.

The two fathers continued to sit totally mute, offering no opinions. This was a woman's issue and they would acquiesce to whatever decision was taken. The burden was ours alone. In fact, it was mine alone, but the reality was that without support, I was helpless to offer any other options or make anything happen.

"I don't think having my child raised by one of our mothers while I go to school will work. I think a child deserves to have a family," I declared, "not a substitute." Was there a third choice?

Would our parents suggest helping us start our family together? But then, he wasn't even suggesting this as an option; why would I think this was even a possibility?

The silence was overwhelming. The truth was Romolo and I wanted to pursue our education. Both he and I were young, scared, and naïve and had no idea how we could raise a child, especially without significant financial and emotional support from our parents. This was not being offered.

I'm truly alone in this terrible moment. He has no suggestions. Neither have they.

The walls closed in on me. I realized there was only one answer: give up this growing living being to a family who could provide the right environment for a happy life. There were no offers of marriage by him, (*I could have insisted, but what good would that do*?) or by parents to support the situation until we got on our feet.

And being a single mother with no financial resources was out of the question.

The next step was clear: make plans to go into hiding until the baby was born. It would be essential to protect my 'good name' and the 'good name' of our family by ensuring our secret was kept from friends, neighbors, and family. The meeting ended in awkward silence. Romolo's parents politely said, "*Buona Sera*," and made their way out the front door. This was no longer a group decision warranting further discussion. The stage was set for the next phase of a long and difficult life journey.

Chapter Two
Nerina and Giannino

Nerina bore her four children in Barete in the province of L'Aquila, a small mountain village northeast of Rome. They lived in the stucco house her husband's parents had built. Each child was delivered by a midwife in the same stark bedroom. Giannino, her husband, had decided a new and better life was waiting for them in America. He had heard stories from a cousin who was already living in the United States. It would be a better life for their school-aged children. They would get a decent education and have more opportunities. They came to New York and started over. The change was dramatic.

Moving to the United States left Nerina without a community, without support or the language to function in it. Her body ached reminding her of her extreme loneliness and emotional emptiness. Her health became her focus and the family suffered along with her as she coped with psychosomatic illnesses. Within a few years of landing in the United States, just about every other year, she would declare her illnesses needed to be looked at by an Italian doctor with whom she would be able to communicate. She would pack up her two teenage daughters, Maria and Angela, disrupting their assimilation into the American way of life, and head back to the mountains outside of Rome, where she would stay for the remainder of the year. The girls would be enrolled in Italian schools. Once again, they would need to acclimate to their native culture. Meanwhile, her husband and the two boys, Romolo and Ennio, would be left to fend for themselves in America.

Then a year later, the two girls and their mother would return, and once again, the girls would re-enroll in the American school and try to readjust to the language, the culture, and the shock of dislocation. Thus, it had been off and on for the last four years.

Her husband wore thick wire rimmed glasses, belying his years of squinting over his work at his tailor shop, focusing on the details of his sewing trade. Behind these coke bottle lenses, his eyes still had a twinkle, and even his wrinkles gave the impression that he smiled on a regular basis…but maybe not as much at home. You could tell he had been a handsome man, with finely carved Roman features. His silver-gray hair was slicked back, revealing a receding hairline. His hands were delicate. His nails were neatly clipped, except for the pinky on his right hand, which had a finger nail of more than a half inch in length, a naturally groomed tailoring tool used to pull threads without reaching for additional help.

His routine was simple each day: work for ten hours alone in his sole proprietor shop on the main street of Port Washington, tailoring, and speaking enough English to interact with his customers. Then come home to drink a tumbler or two of red wine, eat his dinner with the family which Nerina had prepared, and then gather with his *amici maschi* (male friends) from the neighborhood to a small table in the backyard or, in winter, at the kitchen Formica table, to smoke cigarettes, play cards, and drink more wine while his wife cleaned up and put children to bed. By ten o'clock, he would weave his way upstairs to bed and fall asleep in a hazy fog of red wine for another cycle of the same tomorrow. He and Nerina lived side by side in their traditional roles. It was never discussed whether this satisfied either of them. It was just the way it was.

This was the environment in which Romolo was growing up in the United States. He lived with his brother and father almost like three bachelors, while his mother and sisters moved between the two cultures every year or two. This left the boys growing up without much direction, having to figure out this new culture and its values. Regardless, by the time Romolo was eighteen, he was fluent in English and appeared well ensconced in the teenage world of America.

Chapter Three
Innocent Encounter 1963

Romolo walked into the cafeteria, tray in hand with a couple of his friends. They sat down next to my girlfriends and me. He smiled and said,

"Is it okay if we sit here?" in a soft Italian accent, smiling.

I was sixteen. It was 1963. My heart began to pound. I thought it would catapult out of my chest. What was going on here? His warm brown eyes, Mediterranean complexion, and wavy hair were inviting me to keep looking. I was mesmerized. I guessed he stood around five nine; standing my full five-foot two and a half, he looked tall with his trim athletic build made for running.

His two friends awkwardly dropped their trays onto the beige Formica tabletop, laughing with eyes averted from us. They immediately vied for his attention. They spoke loudly, an apparent intentional communication to ensure we could hear.

"Romolo, when's the next soccer practice?"

I learned his name as his friends addressed him; he responded by explaining that the practice was this coming Friday. They whispered and laughed. Occasionally, our eyes reconnected while the pace of my heartbeat increased until it felt like it was bursting.

My girlfriends giggled, watching the silent flirtation unfold. Everything else faded from view except him. An invisible rubber band wrapped around my core, pulling tightly whenever our eyes met.

During the following week, we'd pass in the hallways, and nod at each other. While I focused on my schoolwork, I was becoming increasingly distracted. I couldn't wait to see him again. I decided to do a story for the school newspaper about soccer. I would ask Romolo to be my subject matter expert. This would give me an opportunity to see him again on the soccer field and learn more about him through the interview. I invited my friend Julia to join me to watch him practice.

"Sure, why not? I'll bet Sandra and Rita might want to come too."

Friday, we headed over to the field where the practice was underway. The smell of youthful sweat filled the air. He was just coming off the field for a cold drink when we sat down on the bleachers. He greeted me warmly and I muttered 'hello' back to him. My friends and I watched as he and his teammates darted and raced across the field, knee socks covering their firm calves, leaving lean muscular quads in full view. They raced and darted down the field, moving the soccer ball with their feet as if they had magnets and the ball was made of metal. Their backs were dark with sweat. Their hair was soaked.

The practice went on for two hours and nobody seemed to mind a small huddle of girls sitting in the bleachers, watching their every move. In fact, I think the boys played harder because of it, occasionally glancing over at the bleachers to see if we were looking.

I nervously buttoned up my cardigan. When Romolo took another break to grab a drink, our eyes met intensely for a fleeting moment.

"You enjoying watching the practice?"

"Very much. You have great stamina to run up and down the field non-stop."

"Thanks. It keeps me in good shape, all this running."

He put down his bottle of cold water and charged back onto the field. We continued to watch as the players darted about, heading and dribbling the ball with precise agility: a choreographed athletic ballet targeting the opponent's goal post.

A week later, I returned to the same area of the cafeteria where we had first met, quietly hoping he'd come by and sit at my table. I expected my girlfriends to tease me about the pattern of claiming the same place at the same table. I really didn't care. I arrived early to ensure I could sit at the table alone, when he appeared with his tray and without his friends.

"Hey there. I really enjoyed watching the practice last Friday. You play very well. Listen, Romolo, I'm on the school paper and am writing an article about the game. I'm wondering if I could interview you about soccer and your experience?"

"Sure, no problem," he responded quickly. "We could meet tomorrow and you can ask me your questions?"

I was ecstatic. I would get to see him again and learn more about him. Oh, and yes: I'd gather information to use in my article. The next day, we met again at the same cafeteria table. We agreed it would be better to find a quiet spot where we would be undisturbed.

We headed out the cafeteria door and found a weathered picnic table on a small patio along the back of the school overlooking the playing fields. The golden warmth of the sun felt glorious as we settled in for our conversation. He told me he started playing soccer when he was around five years old growing up in the house his father and grandfather built, in the mountains a few hours northeast of Rome in the Umbria region. He would practice soccer in the dusty courtyard behind his home with his younger brother, Ennio. I asked him about his life in Italy and he described how his mother would cook their meals using herbs and vegetables from her vegetable garden while she watched the boys out the kitchen window.

"Our stucco house was nice but small. We only had one big room downstairs which had a fireplace and a few pieces of old furniture my mother covered with fabric that always reminded of my Nona's dresses."

I couldn't help but laugh at his description.

"Please go on."

"We had a big wooden table at the end, near the kitchen where we ate all our meals. There were three bedrooms upstairs: one for my parents, one for my sisters Angela and Maria, and the other for me and my brother, Ennio. We had no running water except for an outdoor pump."

"Really? No indoor plumbing?"

I had never known anyone to grow up without a bathroom in the house. I began to understand what an adjustment moving here must have been for him.

"We had a big tub for baths that sat on the side of the big room downstairs. Once a week, my mother would get water from the pump outside and heat it on the stove for our bath."

As he spoke about his upbringing, it became clear to me that he cherished things about his childhood and the adjustment to the American way of life was dramatic. His former life was simple but happy. He described his mother cooking in her cement-floored kitchen, rolling pasta dough or forming the polenta into squares, making tomato sauce, the pungent herbal aromas of fresh garlic, basil, and oregano wafting into the courtyard as hungry boys worked up an appetite practicing their soccer dribbling skills under a clear Umbrian sky. He gazed away as if he were inhaling the aromas and smiled with good memories of his early years.

I asked about his father and whether he played soccer with him and his brother. He explained his father did his tailoring in their house. He had a few helpers, but he still worked long hours six days a week.

"He did not have too much time to play soccer with us except on Sundays. We learned about soccer from school or from friends."

He told me whenever his mother asked him to pick up meat from the butcher, Liras in hand, he would skip along the cobblestone streets kicking his soccer ball all the way to the shop. He would exchange the money for meat for their evening meal, and with paper wrapped package in hand, he'd dribble his way back home. Every opportunity was a skill practice, even when doing a mundane errand. He told me how they would find open fields to play a game. They would use rocks and twigs to mark off the playing area. "That is all we had and all we needed to play a game."

For these young boys, owning a soccer ball was the most important thing in their lives. For most kids living in this mountain town, fifth grade was the highest grade they would achieve. Then they would be expected to work, either on the farm or in the village. This was a primary reason Romolo's father decided to move his family to the United States to give his children the opportunity for a better education.

As I interviewed him, I noticed details. His fine fingers were not made for heavy labor, but rather delicate work. He talked about wanting to be a doctor and his love of science and literature. He came to America in 1958 at the age of thirteen, without any knowledge of English.

"This was a very difficult time for me when we first arrived. My little brother and younger sisters quickly picked up the language. For me, it took longer."

"Well, you've done extremely well considering it has only been five years since you arrived!"

I was in awe of his ability. I learned as the months went by and our relationship began to blossom, that he had no interest in his father's tailoring business. He would make something of himself in his own quiet, intelligent way.

I typically took a school bus to the high school that was two miles away. I lived at one end of Baker Hill. He lived at the other. Soon, I was getting off the bus at the bottom of Baker Hill, to walk with him hand in hand the rest of the way. He lived in an apartment over an antique store at the intersection of Baker Hill and Middle Neck Road, where there were small shops and grocery stores; it was the edge of a working-class area where there were rentals, walk up apartments and small houses. My end of Baker Hill was dramatically different: surrounded by large, older homes on well-manicured grounds. It didn't matter. I was blind to it all. His clothes were clean and well pressed. His mother was doing the best she could, while his father was establishing his tailoring business in the next town, leaving early each day, and returning in the dark in time for dinner.

Great Neck is a well-to-do community about seventeen miles east of New York City. In 1963, a significant majority of the population was Jewish, successful upper and upper middleclass professionals, who took it for granted that their kids would go to college and achieve great things. I went to school with Sid Caesar's kids. Perry Como, a crooner from the fifties lived in the next town over. I was surrounded by kids who got televisions and cars if they graduated with good grades, let alone got accepted into college. My middle-class upbringing didn't include this kind of opulence. When I was in fifth grade, we moved to Great Neck from Queens, a lower middle-class environment. I babysat to make money to buy clothes. I got a small allowance to pay for bus fare and extras. I was not part of the Great Neck 'in crowd'. My friends like Julia, Rita, and Sandra were all on the socio-economic fringe, like me, or looked different due to race (Sandra was African-American) or body type (Rita was extremely tall and Julia was quite buxom).

Romolo was also from a very different demographic: a first-generation Italian whose goal of going to college included finding ways to pay for it and working twice as hard to succeed. Meanwhile, the Vietnam War loomed large, threatening to crush dreams and kidnap young men like him by drafting them into the Army. For young men who had no plans to go to college, the military was appealing: the uniforms, promises of training and financial incentives and military or civilian career paths. The war was foreign, but appealed to those who were patriotic without question, or who saw the military as a career, a way to gain new skills or finance for further education later.

For the rest, like Romolo, it was a confusing battle with no end in sight. He had a vision that did not include the Army and I was glad hearing him talk about it.

"I don't understand why America is getting involved. We are not threatened. It seems like it's a foreign war between two countries. Why are we drafting people to fight?"

I couldn't explain it to him, no less to myself.

Chapter Four
Change

Fall came, and I competed and got accepted into the New York All-State Choir. I came home to announce my selection and explained to my parents there would be a concert.

"Do you have a solo or are you just one of the singers?" my Dad asked.

"No, I don't have a solo. I'm in the alto section."

"If we come to the concert, we won't hear you?"

"Uh, I guess not. You'll hear the whole choir."

My father couldn't understand the honor I felt. I was thrilled to have competed and been chosen to join a select group of high school singers from all over the state who would rehearse together and put on a concert that would produce a record. My father had expectations of me that were sometimes beyond reality. If I didn't have a solo, in his mind, being chosen was no big deal. Despite my father's lackluster reaction, life was feeling good. I was fulfilling my interest in music and writing, while dating a boy I had fallen in love with.

November 22, 1963, the choir was rehearsing at a nearby high school, preparing for our concert. Suddenly, the loudspeaker of the school came on with the principal tapping at the microphone.

"Um, testing, testing. Attention everyone, attention please. We have a very important announcement to make. President John F. Kennedy has been shot. We are waiting for further details. All activities for today and this week have been canceled until further notice."

The whole choir gasped. The President had been very proactive in supporting civil rights. The black community respected him and saw him as a guiding light to a new, more equal universe. The whole chorus gasped and began whispering about what this meant. We could hear the whimpering of some of the black girls in the group who were expressing their sorrow over losing an important leader. We were all in shock at the news. Rehearsals were canceled that day to be resumed the following week. We had a war we were afraid of and now a President who had been gunned down in Texas. The world felt upside down in our young minds.

***

On a crisp winter morning of 1963, as Romolo and I walked hand in hand to school, our frozen breath curling in wisps above our heads he announced,

"I got accepted to Columbia University as a premed student with a scholarship!"

"That is fantastic!" I sighed with relief. He wouldn't be too far away and the threat of the draft had been deferred for the next four years. My only thought was,

Maybe this crazy war will be over by the time he graduates, and I won't need to worry about what happens next.

The Vietnam War was taking a turn for the worse, engaging the United States to stop Communist North Vietnam and the Viet Cong guerrillas from overtaking South Vietnam. It was not a popular war and most Americans worried about why we were getting involved. Students, especially young men turning eighteen, were particularly vulnerable since this was when they had to register and possibly be considered 1-A and deemed draft-ready by the draft board.

There were only a few ways to avoid it: get accepted into college, be responsible as the sole provider for your family, or have a medical problem that would exempt you from service. Even then, following graduation from college, they were still vulnerable to being drafted at twenty-one. Graduate school did not exempt them.

We watched nightly news and for the first time in civilization, could see in graphic, horrifying detail the brutality of a foreign war daily on television. Limbs blown off. Young men with shrapnel embedded in their bodies. We heard about neighbor's sons volunteering or being drafted and losing their lives. The fear that this could touch me personally was always there, threatening to unravel my reality.

This had turned into an American War with very little popular support, and everything about it infected our daily lives. Music was written about dodging the draft. Boys grew their hair long as a direct statement against the military crew cut. The lyrics of our music became major political statements from a youth who wanted to see a future without the threat of being sent to war.

Weekly protests were staged with passionate speeches on campus library steps by students who might one day be leaders. Young musicians wrote songs and plucked their guitars in support of young men trying to avoid the draft:

"Sarge, I'm only eighteen,
I got a ruptured spleen and I always carry a purse.
I got eyes like a bat, and my feet are flat, and my asthma's getting worse."

– Excerpted lyrics from Philip Ochs' *Draft Dodger Rag, Appleseed Recordings.*

This war had nothing to do with us. We couldn't feel the threat of communism in our day-to-day lives. We were in a bubble of youth, looking forward to our future. We didn't join the protests. We went to class, and focused on our small world of school, and our all-important relationships. We stood by, quietly agreeing with the protests, but not engaging. We were the silent ones who just wanted to get on with our young lives and avoid the mayhem.

Romolo graduated from high school in June and the following September 1963, he left for Columbia University in New York City. I had only one selfish political thought:

Maybe this terrible brutal foreign-based war will be over and he'll be safe from the draft.

He was just about to turn nineteen, and I was seventeen. I was completing my last year of high school and starting to apply to colleges. The future looked exciting; I was launching my next chapter of independence. Out of the house, and living somewhere elsewhere, my freedom would no longer be questioned or managed. I would become a teacher, and make a life someday with my future husband. I was in love, and the opportunity to express it in physical contact was a strong desire that had never been there before.

There was only one time I had ever been touched by a boy: I was a pubescent girl of around twelve. Walking home from the park with my little brother Philip, a boy I vaguely knew from school hid in wait and pulled me into some bushes in order to touch my breasts. I screamed, "Stop!" and shaking all over, pushed him back, and ran home with Philip, never mentioning that frightening moment to anyone. Now at seventeen, my innocence was leading me to explore the pleasure of mutual touching as a source of enjoyment rather than shock.

When Romolo came back into town from the city on weekends, we were inseparable, spending as much time together as we could with a minimum budget, but who cared? What was important was being together. After a movie and a snack at the local hang out, he'd drive me home in his father's old white Chevy. We'd roll into my driveway, where the outside light would be shining and sit there, talking about school, friends, and the future. Neither of us was eager to say 'Good night'. Then we'd kiss and hold each other tight, feeling the animal tug in our loins. His hands touched me as if I he was embracing a fine sculpture, tracing each curve.

Predictably, the outside light would flash on and off. It was my mother's signal that it was time to come in. She had been watching from the dining room window.

"I can't believe she is doing that! I'll be eighteen this year! Why can't she leave us alone to say goodnight?"

"Let's just find somewhere private," he suggested.

The motor of his father's old white Chevy grumbled as he turned the ignition on and backed onto the road without turning the headlights back on. Once we were down the block, he'd turn on the headlights and pick up speed.

"Let's drive down to the Bay off North Shore Road. The lights are pretty, and it's private and quiet."

How could I say no? My hormones were in overdrive. My heart was beating fast. The sexual tension of two teenagers was palpable. I felt blinded to any other reality. It was as if a huge magnet was pulling me in a direction I had no ability, nor desire to fight.

Once there, we were free to explore this new experience. Neither of us truly understood what we were doing and the potential risks of our naïveté. All we knew is it felt good and we wanted to hold each other close and feel what we were feeling. Little did my mother realize back then that by flashing the outside lights at us while we sat and necked by my own house, she had caused us to find a more secluded place – one that afforded us more privacy than we probably should have had, pushing us further down the road to disaster than if she'd left us alone in the safety of my driveway.

Chapter Five
Turning Point

It was spring of 1964. I had been accepted into the State University College in New Paltz, situated in a small town ninety-miles north of New York City. Soon I would graduate from high school and move on to live in a dorm full of girls, experimenting with makeup and hair rollers, talking about class assignments and boys, while humming to the songs of the Beatles and Rolling Stones blaring on transistor radios. I would live in a cinder block dormitory with ten by twelve institutional gray painted rooms, bunk beds crammed against walls with just enough space to squeeze in a couple of desks, and a slim chest of drawers to share. This would be our new independent haven. Freedom waited.

The cacophony of robins, sparrows, and cardinals outside my bedroom window, had wakened me as if in celebration of the glorious blue sky and my excitement about graduating from high school and leaving for college. Streams of pure clear light poked through my bedroom blinds as I slowly opened my eyes from sleep, watching the tiny iridescent dust particles floating in the morning sunlight.

I woke up feeling queasy. *Did I eat something that is not sitting well? I really don't feel like even getting out of bed!*

Once a month, my Dad would gather the family together to enjoy a family dinner at a local restaurant. My sister Pat, who was twenty-one, my twelve-year-old brother, Philip, and I would pile into the back seat of our car and head out for our ritual family meal. Inevitably, my dad would light up a big brown cigar, in celebration of our outing. At the best of times, he'd crack open the front windows, while my brother, sister and I would suffer the nauseating cigar smoke wafting its way to the back seat like a poisonous vapor.

"Dad, are we almost there?' my brother would whine.

All we could do is hope we'd get there soon so that we could suck in fresh air as soon as the car door swung open in the restaurant parking lot.

"Are you getting up Max? We're going out for our family dinner today and you need to clean up your room."

My mother was surprised to find me curled up in a fetal position still in bed.

"Yeah, I'll get up and clean my room, but I'll pass on dinner out," I rolled over and hugged my pillow against my belly. "Not feeling too good. Not hungry. I think I just want to stay home."

She looked at me quizzically, wondering if I had an ulterior motive.

"You don't have other plans today, do you?" She asked suspiciously.

"No, I don't. I'm just not feeling good. Please let me stay home. I'm going to clean up and maybe have some tea and crackers."

Over the next few days, the queasiness subsided.

"So, do you think you had a stomach virus?" my mother queried a week later.

"Not sure, but I'm glad it passed. I feel a whole lot better, thank goodness!"

For a fleeting moment, I wondered if I had a problem that was bigger than the flu, but I continued to have 'the curse' and felt assured it was nothing.

Prom night in May was simply magical, the final event before graduation and then college.

"Wow, you look beautiful!" was all Romolo could say when I answered the door in my white and silver threaded strapless dress.

"You look pretty good yourself," was my response as I gazed on my handsome boyfriend in a rented tuxedo.

We danced all night, and took pictures in front of a backdrop of vines climbing a fake garden wall set up outside of the gym. Later that evening, we and our friends rushed back home to change into beach clothes, and headed for Jones Beach for a late-night party. It was a magical night to remember. A month later, my family watched as I marched in my graduation gown, beaming. I had been accepted into college and life was wonderful on all fronts.

As summer got underway, my period stopped.

I had never 'really' had sex with him, so I couldn't be pregnant, could I?

After one month without a period, I started to panic. I told Romolo one evening as we sat in his Dad's Chevy in our favorite private parking place overlooking the Bay; his silence was deafening.

"I don't understand it, but I think I'm pregnant."

Our eyes met briefly. Tears welled up and rolled silently down my cheeks, releasing my anguish and fear. He lowered his head, took a deep sigh, and collapsed forward leaning his head on the steering wheel.

"How could this happen? We just fooled around, didn't we?" he exclaimed. Neither of us knew what to do.

"I guess I should tell my mother and go to the doctor," I barely whispered, only half believing what I was saying out loud.

We sat there, paralyzed and unable to speak.

Romolo dropped me off at my house early and my mother greeted me from the living room where she had been reading.

"Max, is that you? You're home early. Everything alright?"

"Mom, we need to talk." I gulped my anxiety and took a deep breath. "I think I have a problem. I didn't get my period this month."

She dropped her book in her lap and her face went white.

"What? Oh, my god. What have you done?"

"I don't know. I'm not sure."

She booked an appointment with the family doctor for the following week. He greeted us in the waiting room and smiled faintly in his crisp white medical coat, placing his hand on my shoulder and ushering us into his office. His look was a combination of pity and empathy. I provided a urine sample and he asked my mother to wait in the waiting room while he examined me. I went through the motions, while my head swam, hoping it was all a mirage. He told us he would call with the results of the test. Two days later, he called and spoke to my mother. She found me in my room and tapped on my door.

"Can I come in? Well, the doctor just called." Her voice was monotone. "You are pregnant. Your father is going be so disappointed. We will need to figure out what to do very quickly before you begin to show. We can't let anyone know about this."

The results slammed me like a door in my face. I was pregnant. *How could this have happened?* I didn't think I had had true intercourse. *I had had my period up until this month, and now I'm being told I'm a few months along!*

Months passed and my period was not coming back. What were my options? I experienced weird cramps and nausea combined for a few weeks off and on. I went over and over the situation in my head. *Yes, we had 'fooled around' but how could that be? I was still a virgin, wasn't I?*

No: I was pregnant. I really was pregnant. It sideswiped me in an era where this just didn't happen to people like me, even though my parents never explained much of anything to me. Ever. I guess they just figured what I didn't know would mean it would never be relevant.

I could remember the day I first got my period. I was only a little more than nine. I came home after a day playing in the park with Philip, and upon going to the bathroom, found spots of red dotting my underwear. I ran to my mother, crying and panicking about the blood I had discovered. I thought I was dying.

"Ah, you're becoming a young lady!" was my mother's explanation.

That was it. The lack of explanation or insight into the most basic of biological processes would not be discussed. The attitude was what we didn't know would not hurt us. Were they ever wrong? We were naïve and that's the way it would stay.

"Just go get some tissues and we'll shop for what you'll need." End of discussion. At the age of seventeen, I was facing a looming set of circumstances without a clue about the emotional journey ahead. I was a good student. My future lay ahead of me like a cornucopia filled with promise. I was ready to study to become a teacher. My future included my boyfriend and I imagined a fulfilling life. This was a total sideswipe for which I was not prepared. The beginning of an intricate web of lies was being formed to cover the shame: some for friends, different ones for relatives, and yet another set for strangers.

"Your father will be very disappointed in you," my mother repeated. "We just have to find a solution." My mother's words pierced me.

What does she think? Why is she telling me how my dad will feel and not about how she feels? Will he really feel this way? What about how I'm feeling?

She projected his opinion effectively to convey how much this would change his view of me: from being the child he saw as having the highest potential, to one who would destroy his hopes and dreams. I was devastated enough, beyond any sensation. I was a failure. It was 1964 and solutions were not easy to come by. Not without a lot of deception and secret, whispered conversations.

Chapter Six
Solution Search

My mother began to look for solutions. We needed to find a way out. She remembered my best friend Julia's mother was a real estate agent, nicknamed 'Kitty', who seemed to have a lot of connections into the community. She decided to reach out to her and confide about the situation. The next day, we drove down the hill to Julia's house to meet with Kitty.

Kitty answered the door in her professional garb: a buttoned up purple peplum jacket with a matching pencil skirt. Her nails were well-manicured and painted blood red as were her thin lips. I'm not sure how she came by her nickname, which sounded more like a soft, warm, cuddly kind of being, not at all like her. I never knew what her real name was.

"Hello. Come in. Let's talk in here," she said in a clipped no nonsense manner. She was around five-foot four, with a commanding presence: her ink black hair fell just below her jaw framing her expressionless pale mask of a face. She waved us into her kitchen, leading the way, her stiletto heels clicking on her marble foyer as if there was a metronome keeping us on pace. She motioned for us to sit on one of the straight-backed chairs at her well-worn, stark wooden kitchen table. The kitchen looked abandoned, as if the last cook had hung up her apron and left a long time ago. I always wondered about Julie's mother and what her story was.

Had she ever been soft like her nickname at one time? I wondered. *How had her life changed to make her seem so hard-edged, cool, and emotionless?*

She lived in her matrimonial home alongside her husband, Jonathan, who was slowly dying of multiple sclerosis. He resided in their living room in a hospital bed with a full time male nurse by his side. If I dropped by to see my friend Julia, Jonathan would be there, pasty complexion, sipping fluid from a glass out of a straw, sitting propped up in his hospital bed, a book in his lap or the television on. A weak 'hello' would be offered as I passed the living room.

Julia's mother lived upstairs in the master bedroom. The walls were painted pale lavender. It was an ethereal enclave away from the dark and depressing reality downstairs. She kept a lock on her door. This was her sanctuary.

I wondered, who she was keeping out. Even Julia never entered. Everyone seemed to have their own space and were living side by side rather than together. Her emotionally barren family life made it difficult for her to wake up to go to school. I would often drop by in the morning, say 'hi' to her bedridden dad, and bolt up the stairs to shake her and tell her to get dressed and ready for school. I felt grateful for my life, and hoped I could influence hers.

A day after the meeting at the kitchen table, Kitty dropped by and handed my mother a vial containing eight egg shaped black capsules.

"She needs to take one in the morning and one at night. It should begin working in two or three days to abort."

I followed her instructions. Nothing happened. By the fourth day, we knew it wasn't working. I went bowling. We tried horseback riding; still nothing happened. Luckily, the last resort – a back alley doctor – was never contacted. There were no more alternatives. It was 1964; all possibilities had been explored. My fate was set. I would have this baby. My mother contacted an organization that provided an escape – a Home for Unwed Mothers.

"We'll be happy to take your daughter. Call us when she's close to seven months and we can make arrangements to register her then."

"Seven months? We can't possibly hide you until then!" she shook her head and muttered, pacing back and forth in our kitchen, trying to think of an alternative solution, while I sat quietly helpless at the bar height kitchen table.

I would have this baby somewhere, but not here, and not at the Home. We needed to keep me safe from scrutiny, away from the prying eyes and nosey inquiries that would inevitably come from neighbors, friends, and family. There were many decisions yet to be made and stories to be invented along the way as I began this life-changing journey. One thing was clear: lying would become a way of life.

"You are not to talk about this with anyone, even your brother and sister. We'll figure something out. No one is to know of this situation."

We began to weave the stories I would need to remember, depending upon the audience. It was a heavy bitter burden that would become a part of my psyche for decades to come.

Chapter Seven
Women of the Times

My mother, Sherley, was an interesting character. There is no doubt her heritage and her youthful experience contributed to her values and attitude. She was a petite woman of five foot one, with auburn wavy hair, and bright blue almond-shaped eyes. She had an extreme wit and an entertaining personality when in front of strangers. Doing community theater allowed this skill to come out. In her later years, you could hand her a glass of orange juice and tell her it was laced with vodka and within a half hour, she would be dancing on tables and having a great tipsy time, just based on our suggestion. She truly was an introverted actress looking for an audience.

She grew up as the first generation in America of Russian immigrants. Her father had died in a fire; rumors had indicated it may have happened because he drank too much. She and her four siblings were still young, and found themselves needing to work rather than complete high school. I often wondered what her life would have been like had she had been able to continue her education and pursue a career. But this was a different era. Despite her upbringing, she pursued night school and eventually got her high school degree. She was the only sibling who accomplished this. She read voraciously.

She had a little business: typing and editing writer's novels, doctoral candidates' theses, and psychologist's confidential client records. We had autographed copies of books from authors such as Lester Velie *(Desperate Bargain: Why Jimmy Hoffa had to Die, and Murder Story)* and Murray Teigh Bloom *(Thirteenth Man and the Man Who Stole Portugal: The Greatest Swindle of All Times)* who thanked her for her editorial capability and devotion to their projects. She conducted her business in our unfinished basement at her desk next to the laundry basket and washing machine, in front of her ink black metallic Remington typewriter. A single bulb hung on a simple wire overhead, her mentholated Newport cigarette, (which would advance her emphysema in later life), formed silver wisps of smoke curling from her glass ashtray. The clatter of eighty words a minute flew across the paper. Her desk was situated just beyond the dirty clothes hamper. An L-shaped old wooden slab with two drawers was her desk: with just enough space for her typewriter and her boxes of onionskin paper, so thin you could see through it. There were boxes of carbon paper you dared not touch for fear of dark blue ink stained fingertips like blood from a crime scene. Whenever we came home from school, we could find her in the basement.

"I'm down in the dungeon if you need me!" she would yell up the stairs, taking pride in her other role as confidant and editor.

Her Russian immigrant mother, Rose, came from Minsk through Ellis Island at the turn of the twentieth century. She hardly spoke English, even after living in the United States for several years. She lived a simple life with her husband, the baker, and their young son in the poor section of Brooklyn, where streets teemed with immigrants scratching a living by providing labor and goods to the community.

While growing up, my mother's neighborhood was filled with the noise of human struggle.

Smoke belched from chimneys and vendors hawked vegetables from carts. Horses and cars competed for the road. Work was demeaning but necessary. Cleaning homes of those who could afford to pay. Rising in the dark before dawn to make bread in the local bakery. Shoe shining on the street. Cutting meat at the local butcher. Dreaming of saving enough to have their own shop someday. There was no need to speak English, just a willingness to work hard six days a week, twelve hours a day.

Rose bore four daughters and a son. By the time the children were barely teenagers, she was widowed with five children, surviving by taking in boarders and doing people's laundry to afford their little walk up apartment. The girls slept in one room. Her son slept on the couch. The boarder got the third bedroom. I often wondered why my mother and her sisters grew up to be extremely prudish. Some conjectured it was because they had inappropriate experiences with male boarders. We never knew. It was another one of those unspoken issues of the time. It exhibited itself in young women who married, but continued to get dressed in the bathroom, rather than in front of their spouses. No wonder they never discussed 'the birds and the bees' with their children.

Sherley, my mother, was the middle daughter. Her real name was Sadie, but when her oldest sister registered her for school, she took the liberty of changing her name to something more American and chose Sherley, misspelling the name with an 'e' rather than an 'i'.

Sherley could swim like a porpoise and gracefully dive. She knew how to ice skate. She could sing. She was an attractive, witty young woman with a fantasy about being swept away from her banal existence to be treated like a princess. She kept a journal to secretly comment on all the available young men in her world who noticed her...or for that matter, didn't notice her, but she wished they would.

This was an era when meeting a young man who had a job was a ticket out of the crowded apartment. She wore hand-me-downs from her older sisters. She dreamed of a better life through marriage. These first-generation American girls looked at a better life as a simple equation: opportunity equals hard work and a little luck marrying a man who could fulfill their fantasy with their own home and children. This post-World War I generation hoped to finish high school, but for many, it was not possible. Getting a job and bringing home money to help feed the family was much more important.

All the children were expected to contribute to the household as soon as they could. This meant quitting school. Sherley did her part and went to work in a hat manufacturer's front office, taking night courses and getting her high school diploma by the time she was twenty-two. She was the only one of the sisters who accomplished a high school diploma.

Journal Entry: September 1936

Went to the beach with my girlfriend Ann. Sammy and George were there and they smiled at us! They're both such great athletes. I've heard that Sammy wants to learn a trade and become an electrician. I have heard that's a great career. He looks like a good catch! We watched them create a human pyramid of forty feet high with a bunch of other guys. Ann and I were in awe of their strength! We're hoping we see them at the soda shop later today. We're probably going to attend the dance at the Coney Island Neighborhood Youth Club later. I'll have to borrow my sister Belle's dress. I have got to look good for this! Maybe I'll meet my prince who will sweep me off my feet and look like Clark Gable!

She met my father Sidney (who preferred to be called by his middle name, Richard or Dick), through the youth club. He played saxophone and was a short, stocky, good-looking man with a gentle soul, and a warm, inviting smile. They enjoyed each other's company and would often hang out at the beach with their friends, piling onto a beach blanket and forming human pyramids for the camera, or hamming it up in a boardwalk photo booth to capture those black and white moments of their youth. She was expressive yet inhibited, goofy yet sexy. She longed for excitement and stability. He was calm, steady, and dependable, but not particularly exciting.

He laughed at her antics, her sense of humor and creative bent. Ultimately, she fell in love and erred on the side of security over excitement. They married just before World War II was declared. A year later, he shipped out with the Navy and she gave birth to my sister Pat while he was overseas. She wrote letters weekly to my father, using her perfect penmanship and her sense of humor to entertain and distract him.

My dad's mother, Florence, had married at seventeen and by the time she was twenty, had two boys: Sidney Richard and my Dad's older brother, Robert. She was a short, solidly built woman with a square jaw, bright hazel eyes, and a hairdo that let you know she had visited the 'beauty parlor' every other week.

"Do you like my Italian bob? It's the latest fashion," she would croon at my mother.

By the age of twenty-six, she was a widow. By forty, she had remarried and was divorced and by fifty; she had married a third time and was again divorced and on her own. She was a demanding personality. In whispered conversations with my father many years later, my mother often conjectured, "Your mother must've created such stress that your father had a heart attack and the other two just ran away!"

Florence owned a women's dress shop on the lower East side of Manhattan. She sold fine clothes in her boutique and attracted well-to-do clients. She had a commanding presence, ushering her clients into dressing rooms to try on the latest styles, flattering them as they posed in front of her full-length mirrors, always ready to give her opinion, whether she was asked or not.

"That lavender taffeta does wonders for your complexion darling. This is one of those classic little pieces that will keep you in the forefront of fashion."

She dressed in the latest designs, and even when she was playing Grandma, visited fully decked out in platform high heels, fully made up with her silver hair in the Italian bob wearing one of her well-fitted suits. Our neighborhood friends often asked us, "Is that *really* your Grandma? She doesn't look anything like ours!"

The reality was she was working very hard to create an appearance of success. Hiding her roots. Denying her humble beginnings which were not unlike my mother's, as a young first-generation American of a Russian immigrant family. With her son at war, meddling in my mother's affairs became her focus.

"What are you feeding the baby? Are you giving her enough naps? When I raised my son, he had a regular schedule."

"That's fine for you, Mom. This is my first child and I'd like to do it my way, if you please!"

"This is how you treat your mother-in-law – with such disrespect? My son should only know you speak to me this way. I hope he comes home soon!"

"I do too. Because he is my husband now!"

The war finally ended, and as with so many married GIs, I was born within the year in 1946: a peacetime baby. My brother arrived five years later. While he was in elementary school, Florence had a stroke at fifty-seven and required help.

"Maybe the best thing is to get her into a nursing home," my mother quickly suggested to my dad. Florence heard about this suggestion and blew up.

"You want to put me away in one of those sanatoriums? No! I want to stay with my son and his family so I can recover! I won't be a bother. When I'm better, I can help around the house."

"Come on dear," my dad was caught in the middle. "Let's try and have her stay with us for a while until she is over her therapy and can function on her own. Give it a try."

My mother seethed like a rattler with resentment, knowing she would be sharing her young husband with his mother. He would be torn between two allegiances.

"If you insist, okay. But I can tell you this is still MY house!"

My dad sat silently, smiled, and shook his head at being in the middle between the two most important and yet warring women in his life. The friction was palpable. We tip toed around the house, avoiding rooms when the two women were together. Florence spent a good amount of time in her room, never getting out of her nightgown, with her television blaring. Occasionally, a local minister dropped by to visit. I can't recall exactly why this was, given she was Jewish. On these days, she would bathe, dress, apply makeup, and do her hair.

"Looks like you're ready for your date, hmm?" My mother couldn't resist noticing how Florence was getting ready because of a man.

"Yes I am. So, what is it to you? At least someone wants to visit with me and finds me attractive," she said as she primped her hair.

"My God, Mom! He's a minister for Pete's sake, not a blind date! When will you stop worrying about your looks and think about your soul? Why not try being a grandmother to your grandchildren?"

"Soul, shmole! What would you know about that? Your kids pay me no attention. You stay home while Dick works six days a week providing for you and the children. You have it easy!"

They often avoided talking to each other, except to discuss meals and shop together for necessities. My dad often came home to a house where everyone was in their separate places, like fighters in the boxing ring after the bell. The wounds were psychological, but visible all the same. One year of this was plenty.

My father found a little furnished apartment by the ocean on Long Island about an hour away in Long Beach, and over a period of a month, convinced my grandmother that it would be better if she had her own place. She relented, "I think you are probably right. I can cook my own meals and not have to argue with your wife anymore…as long as you visit me, dear."

"Of course, I will, Mom." He was a good, obedient son.

The day came and she packed her bags. My father ushered her through the living room and out the front door, as we watched, telling us kids to say goodbye to Grandma and we'll be visiting her real soon. My mother politely said goodbye and wished her luck. Florence looked like a wounded bird whose feathers were ruffled.

As soon as my mother saw my grandmother exit, arms filled with her brown shopping bag of belongings, my dad carrying her two weathered leather suitcases, and drop into the passenger seat of my dad's black 1955 Ford (the one we washed and shined with him every Sunday), my mother closed the front door and slumped on the couch sighing,

"Ah, I can breathe again!"

***

Sherley thrived in the community theater, where she could play character parts with a sense of humor and a variety of accents that tickled audiences and gave her accolades. Dress her up, give her some funny lines and she was on! She transformed into an extrovert with a way with words. She was an introvert, with a cynical view of the world and an expectation that life was not easy. I often got the impression she viewed the world as an interesting, threatening place full of potholes and missiles. A dangerous place, where you could get hurt if you exposed yourself. Better to go with a script you could depend upon.

She had no close friends. Her younger sister seemed to be the only one with whom she spent any time. When she did meet someone new, she usually said or did something that offended, and they disappeared from her life. If she kept to jokes that she had memorized, everything was good. She had no great desire for friends. Audiences? Yes. Close friends? No.

Here we were, trying to determine what to do with my pregnancy, and she had no script, no simple solution. All she knew was our secret couldn't get out given the morality of the day. She needed to protect me (or were we protecting her?) from the world which would pass judgement. There was no turning back. We would write the script as we journeyed down this dark hole

Chapter Eight
Portrait of My Dad

I often wondered what my dad thought while all this was going on. Did he and my mother have secret conversations that were then translated into action by my mother, or was he totally silent and without an opinion, while she did all the problem solving? I will never know. He was a muscular, athletic man of only five-foot six. Richard or 'Dick' as he preferred to be called, always had a twinkle in his bright-blue eyes framed by long, dark lashes. While my mother could go on with vivid descriptions of people and places, my dad spoke in short to-the-point sentences. She was the emotional communicator; he was the factual one.

Despite his short stature, he was accepted into the Navy as a young man to fight World War II and join a submarine squadron. His athleticism and strength got him in. Years later after the war, he still cut a handsome figure as a Navy Reserve member in his crisp, dark, blue uniform, decorated with Chief Petty Officer's colorful medals, and his white cap.

He would march proudly in Memorial Day parades, while we stood by and cheered, waving our flags. He was the short guy in the back. As kids, my sister, brother, and I would get to accompany him to tour battleships when they were docked at port. We were proud of his status as an officer in the Navy Reserve. Once a year, he'd serve a two-week stint on a ship that went somewhere exotic for training and practice, and we'd wait with anticipation to receive his post cards and hear about his experiences when he returned.

After the war, he started several businesses. In those days, anything was possible and young men returned home to become entrepreneurs in every field. He bought a small lunch place with a partner in a blue-collar part of the Bronx. It sat next to a hospital and near a taxi company, which gave him a solid business for all three meals. A simple neon sign on a brick storefront was all he needed. *Good Home-Cooked Food.* An L-shaped counter wrapped two thirds of the room along with two maroon fake leather booths to the left of the front door. It wasn't fancy, but the food was good and fresh. It was the local food place that everyone knew and could depend upon. Stella was his business partner along with Angel Rodriguez, a young Puerto Rican man who was determined to succeed by making a living in the United States.

Dick had learned to cook on the Navy ships and he could easily prepare a roast and turn it into this week's special – just like you'd get at home: not gourmet, but worth the money and tasty. He'd often spend Sunday afternoons sitting at our kitchen table scouring the Sunday paper looking at ads for good deals on meats to purchase for his business, while this week's roast was in our oven being prepared by him to take to the store early on Monday morning. On these Sundays, our home was usually filled with the mouthwatering aromas of a ham or a roast beef to be offered up as the special during the lunch and early dinner hour that week. He'd head out at four-thirty in the morning six days a week to drive to the Bronx to start his day, get the coffee brewing, and meet and greet the early shift of local cabbies and hospital workers who valued the hearty meals and friendly service.

Occasionally, he allowed me to join him on a Saturday to help at the store. I'd get to make the sodas and serve the ice cream from the short end of the L-shaped counter, while he'd take care of the sandwiches, soups, and hot meals from the other side. By two o'clock in the afternoon, after the lunch hour, I'd see him disappear. He'd slip off his apron, slide around the counter and snuggle up in a fetal position in one of the two booths that sat under the luncheonette window facing the street with its red neon sign, to take a nap. It helped me appreciate his long days and how he coped, coming home after seven o'clock most evenings to be served dinner long after my mother had fed us and gotten us ready for bed. He never complained. It was simply his role.

He had strong features just like my Grandmother Florence, softened by a Cheshire cat smile. He was the calm one in the family: not like my mother who could be set off easily into a flap. They were an interesting couple of juxtaposed dispositions. If he arrived home later than usual due to traffic or lingering customers, he could sense my mother's tension. He'd come into the kitchen, where she would be putting his dinner on the table, and in a broad gesture, sweep her into his arms, leaning her backwards, and kissing her.

"How was your day, dahling?" he'd ask in his most romantic voice, knowing that we kids were witnessing all of this and giggling.

"Okay, but your dinner is getting cold!" she would reply, tittering and trying but failing not to acknowledge his attempt at humor. He'd shrug his shoulders and remain silent. If we were lucky enough to witness this romantic gesture, we'd immediately sense the tenseness in the air would dissipate like vapor on a sunny day.

If we complained about a difficult situation or problem, he would launch into his favorite poem to encourage us with a 'can do' attitude:

"Good, better, best. Never let it rest. When your good is better, make your better best."

St. Jerome

Sundays were often family project days. There was always a chore that would bring us together with Dad's orders.

"Okay kids, outside to wash the car, or rake the leaves…"

Every other Monday evening, he'd arrive home even later than his usual seven-thirty. He was committed to visiting our grandmother, who lived about thirty miles away. Florence would prepare his dinner and he'd spend a few hours with her never complaining about his twelve-hour days. He was solid as a rock: dependable and devoted, unlike his older brother Robert, who was never involved and whom we hardly even knew.

On occasions, he'd ask me to help tally the week's receipts from the luncheonette. We'd sit at the kitchen table, and I'd get to enter the daily sales totals into an old adding machine, cranking the handle for each entry, watching the snaking paper tape get longer and longer with each entry and feeling very responsible. I'd tear off the tape, and fold it around the bundle of the week's receipts and with a snap, secure it with a rubber band that no doubt had been harvested off the morning newspaper. He was, after all, a product of growing up during the Depression. He valued not wasting anything, including rubber bands, which typically were harvested and left around doorknobs for easy access. After scribbling the date on the package, he'd lock it in a metal chest where he kept all his receipts ready for his accountant.

"Thank you for helping. You did a good job. The accountant will be very pleased to see how organized everything is." I would beam with his approval.

He was still involved with his luncheonette, putting in the long hours and serving his customers six days a week in 1964, when I found myself pregnant. He was forty-eight, responsible for supporting the economic well-being of his family. The emotional stuff was left to the housewife. He said very little. It appeared he left the responsibility to my mother to find solutions and deal with the details. It's just the way it was.

In his early fifties, he decided to sell his business and buy a franchise, selling contracts and delivering services for weed and fertilizer treatments of residential lawns. This was a three-season business. During the winter, he could sit back, but instead, offered his services as a courier. We lived in a suburb where there were plenty of lawns and people were gladly willing to spend money to keep their property looking good. His friendly manner and business sense made it easy for him to grow the business and hire others to do the physical labor. He was a great role model for working hard and a 'can do' attitude.

This was a dramatic lifestyle change for him; he no longer left the house at four-thirty in the morning. In fact, he no longer commuted anywhere. He bought a nice car for his sales appointments. His office was in our house and he could start work at eight in the morning and have dinner with us each evening. He went out in the middle of the day for sales appointments. In effect, he invaded my mother's territory, or at least that is how it was perceived by her at first. It took some adjustment since her whole routine was disrupted. Her job as housewife and mother needed to be recalibrated to include him in her plans.

By his mid-fifties, he decided to retire and passed the business on to my brother. He quit smoking, took up tennis as a full-time sport, and bought a motorcycle. He took a course to learn how to use a computer and managed his stocks on a regular basis. He had paid his dues and decided he was going to reap the rewards. Just as his life got better, my mother's life took a turn for the worse as her emphysema took hold, making it harder and harder to breath without lugging an oxygen tank around. It was almost as if his optimistic 'can do' attitude had set him up for a fulfilling retirement, while my mother, whose world often felt threatened and vulnerable, willed herself to have a difficult time in her later years. Watching the way my parents handled the

Chapter Nine
Transition I

Dreams are supposed to reflect something about your life: whether fears or desires. Mine was a recurring one when I was around seven or eight years old. The images are still crystal clear. I'm visiting a local corner nickel and dime store that's going out of business. The owner, a balding man with kind eyes and dusty colored skin, tells me he is getting rid of inventory and since he's known me for a long time because of my weekly bubble gum purchases, he wants to give me a special gift.

We walk to the back of the dimly lit store, crammed with school supplies, canned goods, and old magazines. He climbs up on his store ladder to the fifth shelf and brings down a gray cardboard box with Chinese lettering all over it. Inside the box are six pairs of paper and plastic wings.

"I bought these for Halloween a few years back, but not many got sold," he lets me know. "Here, why don't you take them and see if they're of some use to you this Halloween."

In my dream, I take them home, slip one wing onto each arm and make circular motions like the squawking crows I've seen flapping around our neighborhood, perched on branches of old maple trees.

I soon get the hang of how to keep them on, and begin practicing jumping off chairs, to see if I can get airborne. And then one day, in my dream, I try them from my front steps and I take flight! I'm seeing the world from a bird's perspective and it's spectacular. The air is clear and the clouds are vapors shimmering in a delft blue sky.

As I travel, I look at the earth and see giants and witches moving about down below, wreaking havoc. It is now clear why I am flying. I will swoop down upon these evil forces and force them to stop their pernicious ways. For many months, I would close my eyes to fall asleep and resume this unusual dream, as if I were reading the *Adventures of Flying Maxene*. Was this a message about my life? How could I turn evil into good and rise above all the dangers ahead?

I thought about this dream as I sat in a daze, listening to my mother talk about the need to send me away, somewhere, *anywhere* so no one would see me as my belly began to swell. I had hopes and dreams, and now I was fecund with life, while everything about my existence had come to a full stop. On occasion, I would fantasize about having the baby and marrying Romolo. I played with names, assuming it would be a girl. I landed on Mona or Lisa in my romantic haze. But I had no wings to take me above the fray. My mother quickly began planning.

"We'll find a place you can go to until the baby is born. You can't stay here; we can't let anyone see you. Everyone expects that you're going to college in September."

Her thinking out loud continued. She took it on like a project to be solved. My father was silent and in the shadows of these discussions. My brother was too young to know; my sister was told not to talk about it with anyone. The secret couldn't get out.

"I spoke with our neighbors from our old neighborhood, and they are willing to have you come live with them until they can help you find a place of your own and have the baby," she announced excitedly.

The Hirsh family lived about 70 miles away in the small town of Newburgh. Mr. and Mrs. Hirsh were in the real estate business and they would find a place for me to rent.

"How will I afford this?" I questioned my mother.

"Mr. B, the lawyer, is taking care of the bills," she replied.

Weeks prior to this conversation, the tentacles of this tree of lies began to expand, winding their way through a maze of angles depending upon the audience. My mother had desperately sought solutions. She had discussed 'the situation' with one of her sisters who worked at a dress shop where she had a colleague whose husband was a lawyer and 'dealt with these kinds of things'. My mother got his telephone number and made an appointment. She referred to him as Mr. B.

I had graduated from high school, not even realizing I was pregnant, and had expected to start college in September. I was truly in limbo the summer of 1964, consoling myself by listening to the radio, watching Philadelphia teenagers dance and the latest rock 'n' roll stars perform on *Dick Clark's American Bandstand*, talking on the phone with Romolo and laying low, waiting to be told what comes next. I would no longer be starting college in the fall, unless somehow, this 'situation' changed. We had explored all options, and nothing had worked. Now the only solution was to hide me somewhere so no one would know anything about my condition.

Once the 'situation' was over, I could return home and begin my life again, weaving additional lies to cover my tracks. All of this meant I was moving toward finding a way to give this growing living being up for adoption. It was a surreal time where emotions were deadened. It was as if I were in a haze moving forward without feeling. Invisible. I expected to wake up and find the witches and giants had been slain, and life would be back on track again. But, every day I woke up to the movements in my belly reminding me there was no turning back.

One day in early July, my mother woke me up and announced I needed to dress nicely.

"We are going to a meeting in New York City today to meet with the lawyer, Mr. B, who will help us arrange the adoption of the baby," my mother announced. "He is the husband of a woman who works with my sister Evelyn who deals with these kinds of situations. She gave me his number and I called and made an appointment for us."

We entered his large office with an enormous mahogany desk. The lawyer, Mr. B, a tall, elderly man in a gray suit with thinning hair, a gruff demeanor and an icy gaze, welcomed us. I felt dwarfed by the large bookcases full of legal tomes. He asked us to sit down and immediately focused on speaking with my mother. I had met the wolf and I was the chicken in the coop. His behavior made it quite clear I was invisible as he discussed the 'arrangements' with my mother. He already had identified a couple who were interested in adopting the baby.

"So, this child is from a mixed heritage?" he asked.

"Yes, I suppose so," my mother replied. "My daughter comes from a Jewish-American family and the father is first-generation Italian American."

"Well this should not matter, since according to Jewish tradition, it's the heritage of the mother that counts in these cases," he assured us.

He had asked my mother to supply a photograph of the mother and father of the unborn child. She pulled out my prom picture and handed it over. There I was, in my strapless white dress with the silver threads; he was decked out in a tuxedo, his dark, wavy hair neatly combed. Both of us were beaming. My heart skipped a beat and my stomach was in a knot. A happy moment now was representing a reference point for a life-changing event.

"Nice looking parents," he murmured to my mother, continuing to ignore my presence. I expected at any moment he would lick his chops. I sat in the burgundy leather chair across from his massive desk and gazed around his office; a family photo sat on his credenza, which I concluded was of him, his wife, and a young couple (I guess one of them must have been his son or daughter?) with a little girl, as well as framed pictures of landscapes.

"Young people think they're in love at this age, but it is in reality only sexual," he commented, gazing past me as if I were a manikin rather than a living breathing person. "I can assure you, the adoptive parents are quite willing to help with all living and medical expenses. All we need is a healthy baby, and I will make all arrangements to take care of everything," he told my mother.

My fate was set: I was to be sent away, hidden from all whom I knew, produce a baby, and resume my life. I could start school the following spring and make up lost time. It all sounded so logical. It was emotionless. There was no other path to explore.

The questions started bubbling up as the plans were being put in place. My mother and I drove back home. As we drove past my high school and up the hill toward our house, she began to think out loud about how we would keep all the stories straight; my head was spinning.

"We need to think about how we will answer all the potential questions from friends, neighbors, and family." She began to develop 'what if' scenarios and plausible answers for all potential questions. Lies upon lies were created for different audiences. It was merely a matter of keeping it all straight, depending upon who asked.

*Question: **From relatives and friends:** Why are you home from school in the middle of the school year?*

Answer: I contracted mononucleosis and needed time off to mend. I plan on making up the time by going to school in the summer.

*Question: **From students at the school:** What have you been doing all year instead of going to school?*

Answer: I was working, of course!

My goal was set: graduate with my class in 1968. Since I had deferred starting college until the following spring, it would mean I would need to go to school year-round for two years, to make up the half year I had missed. Then maybe the questions would finally stop.

I packed my bag and left my home, appearing to be headed off to college, around the same time my high school graduate peers were packing to head off to college in early September 1964. I was now 'officially off to school', as far as any of my neighbors, relatives, and friends were concerned.

My mother and I arrived at the Hirsch's in September of 1964 with my one bag of belongings. Their home was an unassuming ranch on an acre of land. Mrs. Hirsch answered the door, while her husband stood in the hallway behind her, ready to welcome us.

"Come on in. Let me show you your room,"

Mrs. Hirsch said softly as she gently touched my arm.

"Are you hungry? Would you both like some tea or coffee and cake?"

"No thanks, we had lunch before we drove up. I'll need to get back soon. My husband and I appreciate your willingness to help," my mother said.

Following some polite conversation, and a tour of the room where I would stay, she hastily said good-bye and soon was on her way back to our family home.

It had been a stressful, lackluster summer at my parents' home; now I would be provided a haven and a routine that gave me structure to my falling apart world. Mrs. Hirsch was a sweet and motherly woman with kind, sad, warm, brown eyes that belied her own life's tragedies. She addressed me in quiet tones, showing concern and giving me chores to occupy my day, including instructing me on how to prepare dinner, while the couple went off to work at their real estate office. I had a role, and they were happy to help.

Mr. Hirsch was a tall, pleasant man with a dark, handle bar mustache. The couple had left our old neighborhood after their two-year-old had succumbed to brain cancer. The memories of their house were too much for them, and they moved away with their three daughters shortly after their young son's funeral. One of their daughters was my age and had just started college. They were a caring couple who knew what family suffering was all about. They showed empathy with my situation, given I was their daughter's age, and viewed helping me as a way to give back to neighbors who supported them through their difficult time.

While at their home, I felt productive and valued after many dark and depressingly slow motion months at home. I learned how to make several dishes with Mrs. Hirsch's coaching, and relished the freedom and peace of their home during the day.

"Are you okay dear?" she would call from her office during the day, checking in on me and seeing if I needed any further instruction on the preparation of the meal or other chores.

I felt free to take pleasure in the outdoors and pick fresh vegetables from their small backyard garden. It was a wonderful respite from the stresses I had recently endured, except when their daughter called from college. The air became tense as they motioned to me to be silent as they talked with her about her college life. It was a reminder of what I was missing. Out of respect for me, they never revealed to their daughter that I was at their house. The Hirschs were not judgmental and I appreciated their support. Soon it became apparent this arrangement was only temporary.

"I'm afraid you can stay only until the first college break at Thanksgiving. Our daughter Lena, you remember you used to play with her at our old house? She will be returning home from college and we know how important it will be that she doesn't see you this way," Mrs. Hirsch spoke with embarrassment, not sure how I would take the announcement.

"We'll make sure we've found a place for you by then."

I thought to myself, *Mrs. Hirsch was just taking care of her own branch of the ever-growing tree of lies and I suppose protecting me.*

I would go further into hiding. I called home to let my mother know about the pending move.

"Mom, it looks like it's time for me to leave here. Lena is coming home and the Hirschs need me to move. They told me they're going to find a place for me to live," I reported.

"Yes, and I realize you have never lived on your own, so I'm thinking we need to find a roommate for you," my mother announced.

It was clear she and Mrs. Hirsch had already spoken and this was no news to her. I wasn't sure what to give thanks for except I had a support system to help me move through the web of deception, step by step. "What do you think about your friend Julia as your roommate? I called her and she has agreed to live with you once you have your own place, until the baby is born. We've offered her some money and she intends to find a job while she lives with you." I sat listening:

realizing yet another person would now be involved in my life which I had little say in.

"I guess it's okay," was all I could say and slumped into the kitchen chair.

Julia had not planned her future, and had not applied to college. She jumped at the opportunity to leave her dysfunctional family home and be independent. We had always teased her about how much older she looked with her buxom figure. Now she would get to find out what it was like to live on her own, work, and be treated like an adult. This appeared to be a win-win for all concerned. Julia got to escape for her reasons, while I was to do my disappearing act and would not have to live alone.

I imagined strangers in the small town where I would be living wondering: *who is she and where is her husband?* We came up with an answer: I was a young bride; my husband was in in the military and over in Vietnam, and would not be here for the baby's birth. *Sounded logical to me. How could anyone question this answer anyway?* The branches of the lies were beginning to leaf out, creating more shadows in my life, vulnerable to the winds of circumstance. It was a constant exercise to stay alert and keep the stories straight.

"We've found a place for you to live!" Mrs. Hirsch declared one morning in early October. "We're going to see it this afternoon and make arrangements for the lease."

The budget necessary to support my new living arrangements was never discussed with me. It was clear the lawyer Mr. B and the adoptive parents were taking care of everything. It was out of my control. The rent check would come to the landlord from Mr. B. It was the only place I would be shown. The month-to-month lease was arranged and I moved in; all I needed to do was pack my one suitcase with clothes and some toiletries. Julia would be joining me in the next week. This was where I would live until the baby was born.

"Here we are!" Mr. Hirsch declared after we drove through the older part of town and turned down an alley. I looked around and didn't know what to say. The furnished apartment was situated off a gray gritty street behind a used appliance store and down a laneway. The street housed several small old retail stores with peeling paint around their windows and doors that had seen better times. Some storefronts were vacant with boards across the aging windows and FOR RENT posters pasted across them. Some had apartments on the second floor, while others, like the one I was being shown, were behind the storefront with its own entrance off the alley.

The apartment had a large eat in kitchen with yellowed linoleum, faded wallpaper with daisies and lime green watering cans on a pale-yellow background, and dim fluorescent lighting. There was a white kitchen table and two matching chairs squeezed up against a wall and across from an old stove, a chipped enamel sink, and a small apartment sized refrigerator that was my height. It was the first time I could see the top of a refrigerator.

The living room was furnished with an old brown couch, a large dark blue over-stuffed chair, a wooden coffee table that had many coffee rings on its surface, and an old black and white television set on a black metal stand. The room was a good size and stretched across the entire back of the apartment. Behind it down a narrow gray hallway lit by a single bulb hanging from the ceiling was a small bedroom with two twin beds, one on either side of the room. Next to the bedroom off the hall was a small bathroom with a salmon pink sink, toilet, and tub. The floor in the bathroom was white and black tiles. The only two windows in the apartment were in the bedroom and they looked out onto a back alley; we would keep the roller blind down and the thin gauzy curtains pulled across the window. It wasn't exciting, but it was private and away from prying eyes.

"Well, we'll say goodbye now," Mrs. Hirsch declared. "You have our number. Let us know if you need anything." They each gave me a warm, meaningful hug, and exited awkwardly.

Soon after helping me settle in and unpack some basic groceries that we had picked up from the local grocer, my mother turned to me, pulling something wrapped in blue tissue paper out of her pants pocket.

"This is something you should wear. It will help you to avoid questions from people."

She handed me a plain gold-plated wedding band. This would help support my story, if I could only continue to keep all the stories straight. I would make no friends and keep to myself. I was now officially banished from home, hidden from all who knew me. I had become invisible and was now pretending to be someone else.

Chapter Ten
A Hidden Life

I settled into my new routine. My mother came to visit after the first few days as I accepted my new reality and helped me shop for more groceries and basic household things I would need. Mrs. Hirsch had recommended a doctor and we made an appointment for later in the day.

"I think you should be having this baby sometime in late January," the doctor told us.

This meant I had about three months to get through.

My mother drove me back to the apartment and let me know my friend Julia would join me the following week. After a day of being busy, she hugged me good-bye and left to make the two-hour trip back to our home. Julia arrived the following week and quickly settled into a routine.

"So, this is it, huh?" She walked around the rooms, both excited to be out of her parents' house, but underwhelmed with the look of the place.

"Yup, this is it. Not great but it's private."

In the following days, she found a job waitressing at a nearby luncheon place and was gone most afternoons and into the evening. I soon realized the arrangement benefited her by getting her out of her mother's house, and I suppose, having someone there overnight was a good idea. Besides, the arrangement included paying her a small amount each month. I assumed the money came from the arrangement that the Mr. B had made with the adopting couple.

I busied myself learning to cook for the first time. My mother had always been obsessive about her kitchen. It was her territory and somehow, teaching her kids about cooking was like giving up her expertise: it threatened her identity. She did not teach us anything about cooking; my only kitchen duty was making pancakes from a *Joy of Cooking* cookbook on the occasional Sunday morning. I watched television. I read. I cleaned. I shopped and took walks. I spent a great deal of time alone, thinking.

If I can just keep reminding myself that this decision is best for the child, will I believe it in my heart? This movement inside of me is real. A baby is growing in there. Do I have any choice? Was this a decision? Will my banishment be something I can reconcile? Am I being selfish? It is for the good of the child.

I often sat in the stillness of the apartment thinking about my fate. I was biding my time until the baby was born. The enormity of the void I was facing was like a boulder whose weight pressed down on my being. I often felt like I was living in slow motion, watching myself. Within the first two weeks of my banishment, the phone rang and I slowly picked up the receiver.

"Hello?"

"Hello? How are you? I'm at school and I got your message with your new number from my roommate about moving into your own place." Romolo spoke hesitantly, not sure of what mood I would be in.

"Yes, I'm here by myself. How is school?

"Oh, it's okay," he responded quietly. "How is your apartment?" I could tell there was a guilty quality in his voice. His life had resumed, while mine was on hold.

"It's old, but I guess it's okay. My friend Julia is supposed to live with me, but she's not here very much. Will you visit soon?"

The sun was slowly setting, throwing gloomy shadows across the linoleum as I sank into the old blue chair, positioned like an embryo, legs curled, listening to his voice, trying to believe he still cared.

"Sure, I will try, soon. I'll find out which bus I can take from the city, or I'll borrow my father's car. It all depends on the soccer schedule. I'll let you know."

Even though we were separated geographically, we continued to stay in touch, calling on a regular basis. There was no discussion about what would happen. It was a *fait accompli*. We behaved as if we were convinced we were doing the best thing for the unborn child, motivated by a mixture of guilt, and some sort of love.

Romolo visited three weeks after my move into the apartment. We embraced as he entered the living room. Tears of silent relief poured down my face, releasing the pent-up tension I had carried around for months, as I muttered,

"I'm so glad you came."

His visit was a bittersweet respite from my banishment. Someone who I thought would understand better than most what I was going through, and yet was not able to help, except to be there. He visited every couple of weeks, staying the night.

Soon after Julia moved in, she began to disappear on weekends to spend time with a cousin of hers out of town. I suspected they were developing a secret and forbidden relationship; she refused to discuss it with me, and I decided better not to ask.

On those weekends, Romolo and I had the apartment to ourselves. We would take long walks into town, avoiding main streets. It's not like I knew anyone, and therefore the possibility that someone would question who he was or what was my situation, was unlikely. I was a stranger, who only needed to answer questions of the landlord or the local retailer who saw me each week, alone, buying enough food for myself. Otherwise, I truly operated as a wraith, almost invisible to most, functioning day to day unnoticed.

My father called to see how I was doing, and on a several weekends came alone to visit. (I was told by my sister years later, she had also visited, but quite frankly, this experience has been lost from my memory). These visits by my father were welcomed, especially after my mother had told me how disappointed he was in me. In retrospect, these were significant times when we sat in a local restaurant over dinner and spoke about the news, and what was happening with our family.

"I bet you're looking forward to starting college," he'd say.

"Yes I am. It will be hard and I guess I'll need to make up time, but I can do it."

"I know you can." He smiled his warmest, although he tended to be unemotional at the best of times. He never appeared judgmental. He simply expressed genuine interest in how I was doing. It was a unique period when I spent more one-on-one quality time with him than ever before. It deepened our relationship in a way my mother could never quite comprehend. We were two adults enjoying each other's company. I felt pardoned and respected, rather than rejected. It built a bridge between us that would last the rest of our lives.

During the second month of my isolation, I received a call from Mr. B.

"How are you doing?" he inquired.

"I'm okay," I responded emotionless.

"Good, I'd like to come and visit," he stated in a perfunctory manner, as if he were ordering a ham and cheese sandwich or arranging for a court date. It was not a request. It was a declaration that he would be coming.

Mr. B showed up two days later in the afternoon of a cold and rainy November. The sky looked dark and ominous. The remaining leaves on the trees whipped and rattled like dried newspaper ready for the fire. I would have preferred to stay in bed, but had dressed myself and cleaned up the kitchen in time for his visit. Julia, as usual, was off working. The doorbell rang and I hesitantly answered it. This was the first time Mr. B would communicate with me directly without another person in the room. My nerves were jangled. He stood in the doorway, a tall man with a dark gray brimmed hat glistening with rain and a black raincoat. I took both from him and hung them on a hook beside the apartment door.

"Come on in," was all I could mutter without smiling. I was not happy to see him, but felt it was my duty.

We sat at the kitchen table as he attempted to make small talk. *This visit is nothing more than his way to assure himself that the 'arrangement' was successfully underway and all parties will get what they want,* ran through my head.

"You are looking well. It is quite a miserable day out there, isn't it?"

"Yes, I suppose," I replied.

"How are you feeling? Are you seeing your doctor regularly?" he asked.

"Yes, of course." I couldn't believe he would think otherwise.

"I have confirmed arrangements with a very nice couple who are ready to adopt the baby as soon as it is born," he declared in a matter of fact manner.

I guess he expected me to react with some sort of joy. Instead, I sat there staring at him, emotionless. My insides were knotted. He reached into his jacket and pulled out a dog-eared brown wallet. He spread the billfold and dug around in it with his long hairy fingers.

"Here: treat yourself to something nice," he declared, and held out a ten-dollar bill.

I sat there unable to speak. I felt cheapened being offered money by this man, a man who was completing a transaction without empathy, without acknowledging me as a human being. I made no move to accept the money, and he awkwardly laid the bills on the old wooden table, realizing my stony gaze was not being lit up by his offering. He sat there awkwardly.

"That's okay. You can keep your money," was all I could say.

"No, it's for you; I insist. Take it and buy something for yourself."

He pushed the kitchen chair back, making a scraping sound, and got up from the table moving toward the door. He had visited for all of ten minutes.

"Well, I'll be going now," he mumbled in a low growl, "I need to get back to my office before the traffic starts." He grabbed his hat and coat off the hook by the door and hastily said good-bye, averting his eyes from my gaze as he pulled open the door and retreated into the laneway.

"Goodbye," was all I could mutter as I quickly closed the door behind him and secured the deadbolt.

His mission was accomplished. I looked healthy and was growing the prize for which his clients were paying him. *Good-bye, and please don't come back.*

Chapter Eleven
Transition II

The holiday season was in full force. Snow was gently floating like fine goose feathers from the sky, covering everything with a glistening white blanket. Even the old boarded up abandoned shops took on a more cheerful demeanor with the snow piling on their roofs. The gusts of white crystals swirled and landed on the wool hats and puffy coats of children with their families, shopping for Christmas presents on the main street. They skipped and laughed as they trolled the stores for gifts.

Romolo borrowed his father's car and came to visit the day after Christmas. By this time, my girth had expanded and I was slowing down as my back began to ache if I walked too much. I woke up in the middle of the night feeling very uncomfortable, and soon realized I was in the early stages of labor.

"How is this possible? I was told I have until January before I'm due!" I groaned with the next wave of contractions.

By the morning, it was obvious, the contractions were stronger and more often. I was going to have the baby sooner than anyone had expected. I needed Romolo to leave.

"You need to go! I need to call my mother!" I could not risk having him found at the apartment.

"Okay, I'll leave," he exclaimed, and hurried out the laneway to the car.

Luckily, Julia was there and we immediately called for a taxi to the hospital and called my mother to let her know. The father of this child would not be there when it was born.

We arrived at the hospital, and I was asked to sit at the registration desk and fill out paperwork, even though I was experiencing the searing pain of labor. I had been instructed by Mr. B to leave blank the space where the father's name was supposed to go. *Check: another lie.*

This child has no father on record. Just me. Was this so there were fewer risks of repercussions later?

Once the paperwork was completed, I was put in a wheelchair and whisked to the labor area, where I was quickly changed into a hospital gown. Within an hour, the contractions increased and I was wheeled into the delivery room.

"Just relax and don't push right now," the nurse in a crisp white uniform advised without looking directly at me.

The pain began to increase, gripping me around the midsection. An epidural was quickly administered, numbing me from the waist down. The labor mirrors that were perched above the delivery table were pushed out of the way, shielding all opportunity to see the birth from my view.

Within a couple of hours, my baby was born: a healthy, seven-and-a-half-pound girl. Before I could even see her, she was whisked off to the nursery, and I was wheeled in the opposite direction to a private room. It was a blur of nurses' visits and silence. There were no suggestions that I would get to see the baby. She was protected from me, and I suppose I was protected from her and the natural love and bonding that would have flowed was blocked.

Soon however, nature took over: milk began to fill my breasts, reminding me of the weight of this event every waking hour as the discomfort grew by not nursing my child. I felt full and yet empty, physically uncomfortable and emotionally drained.

On the fourth day, my mother came to take me home, bringing with her the yellow and white layette Mr. B had provided. On this, my final day in the hospital, the floor nurse let me know I would get to dress the baby. This would be the first and only time I got to see her. I dressed and waited with my mother for the nurse. My daughter was brought into my room for the first time and placed on my bed. I stood and stared at her, taking in an image that would need to last a lifetime.

She was perfect, with a silky cap of caramel brown hair and long, dark eyelashes. I carefully dressed her in the crocheted layette, unable to speak. I bent over and kissed her gently on the forehead, and felt the rose petal softness of her pink skin. She smelled like that unique baby powder aroma. The nurse brought a wheelchair into the room.

"It is hospital policy that the mother needs to be wheeled out of the hospital with her child, for safety and security reasons," she advised, knowing that this was the first and last time I would be with the baby.

I sank into the wheelchair, and she gently placed my daughter in my arms, a swaddled bundle of seven and a half pounds of warmth, and wheeled me through the hallways, passing excited fathers ogling babies through the nursery window and florists busily delivering congratulatory bouquets and balloons to mother's rooms. I couldn't take my eyes off her.

We exited the hospital's front door. Mr. B was already waiting on the street in an idling taxi. I was wheeled through the automatic hospital doors, and he quickly jumped out of the vehicle and rushed up the stairs to the front of the hospital to meet us.

"Hello. Good to see you," he declared, and at the same time, swooped down and lifted the baby into his arms. He turned and quickly darted back to the taxi, as he said good-bye.

"I'll be in touch soon," were his parting words. I stood up uneasily, the world a blur around me.

The nurse took the wheelchair, saying, "Good luck," and quickly retreated through the glass doors. My mother and I walked to the parking lot in silence.

"Why don't you get in the back seat and lie down," she suggested.

I got in the back seat and sat upright, refusing to lie down. I was not sick. I was overwhelmingly sad and empty. Totally empty. Void of emotion. Frozen in time. *Why should I lie down? I'm not feeling physically sick, just emotionally wasted. Why am I in the back seat? Does she want to make sure I'm still not seen when we get back to my home? Perhaps, this makes it easier for us to drive in silence and not have to talk to each other. What was there to say, anyway?*

We left Newburgh that day forever. My mother had gone to the apartment earlier and let Julia know she could stay through the month, packed my clothes and came to the hospital to pick me up. Now we were headed down the highway and driving in deafening silence, to arrive at my family's home two hours later. My brother was at a friend's; my sister was in her room; my father was working. It was a perfect time to arrive and quietly resume my life with a new set of stories to remember for family, neighbors, and friends.

"If anyone around here asks why you're home in January, we'll just explain that you got mononucleosis and will be home to recover before returning to school this spring."

Since I blocked some memories out of my mind, the fact that my sister knew about my situation was completely lost from my memory, while my young thirteen-year-old brother had been told I had come home from college to recover from an illness. No matter: I never had a conversation about my situation with either of them. It is amazing to me that even now, I do not recall her visit with me while I was in hiding. She has told me we spent an hour or two over lunch in my small apartment, and tearfully hugged and said good-bye when it was time for her to go home. Years later, she revealed how bad she felt to leave her younger sister all alone, banished from our family's home. Sometimes painful memories get buried, never to resurface.

The veil of silence had been lowered and was never broken. My mother had told my sister where I had gone and why, but had emphasized the need not to talk about it. We lived together in our family's house for three months following my exile, but what had happened, and how I felt was never broached nor advice given. It was truly the elephant in the room and taboo to raise the topic. The veil of silence covered me up and stifled my words.

Chapter Twelve
Transition III

My return home was a period of blurred existence. I busied myself around the house helping with chores and generally lying low. In the first few weeks, I was reminded daily of my loss with the discomfort of milk continuing to fill my breasts with no child to suckle. To the world of friends and family, I was home from college, ill with mononucleosis. I had no appetite to see or speak to anyone. I was in a fog of final penance for my sin.

I had changed my college start date from September 1964 to March of 1965 so that I could begin the process of making up for the loss of six months and graduate with my college class. It was a race to remove any explanation of where I had been; I could finally eliminate the lies. Once I had made up for lost time and graduated with my class, I would no longer need to explain my late college start. My goal was to erase the story from my repertoire for good.

Around the second month of living with my parents, my mother informed me there were papers to sign so that the adoption could proceed. I can't recall signing, but I guess in my postpartum haze, we made one last trip into the city to see Mr. B.

"It's best this way," my mother commented as we drove back from the city. I kept my eyes focused on the road, unable to respond. However, thoughts raced through my head. *It's hard to imagine being a parent when I'm only eighteen, so I guess it was the right thing to do. I just hope this feeling of sadness subsides.*

Romolo and I continued to clandestinely see each other whenever I had an excuse to be out of the house. The pull was too great. Occasionally, I would be asked to baby sit for a neighbor and would gladly take on the assignment for the money and the privacy it afforded us. It had been tacitly understood he was off limits. After dark, comfortably ensconced in a neighbor's house, with their children tucked into bed, he would stealthily arrive at the back door, so that we could spend time together. What were we motivated by? Love? Guilt? Sex? Loneliness? All of it? I'm not sure we could explain it if we tried.

Chapter Thirteen
Good Will

I anxiously counted the months before I would resume my 'normal' life and start college in March of 1965. It was January and my Aunt Evelyn had called to spread the news that her daughter, my older married first cousin Cindy, had just announced her first pregnancy. Only a few weeks following this announcement, my mother received the terrible news that her brother Jack had a massive heart attack and died at fifty-two. He was a talented saxophonist and had a band that played at all kinds of events and in local bars. My mother took it hard.

"He was so young. His lifestyle didn't help any, with all the late nights and probably too much alcohol. What a shame he'll never get to see his sister's grandchild."

Two days later, we visited my uncle's apartment to pay our respects. My Aunt Lila was sitting shiva, the Jewish tradition equivalent to a wake without the coffin. We arrived with some baked goods and rang the doorbell, shuffling and whispering in the hallway of the three-story walk-up. A family friend answered the door and ushered us in.

We entered the apartment solemnly. The air was perfumed with floral bouquets placed throughout the room. Lila was sitting on one of her dining room chairs at the end of the living room, dressed in black. Her coal black hair was pulled into a neat bun.

Her pale crystal-blue eyes were swollen from crying. The whites had a pink tinge. She looked wan and drawn. My mother handed her our baked goods, and with a sweeping motion, put her arms around her sister-in-law. They held each other for a full minute. The only sounds were quiet sobs from both bereaved women.

I was touched by the scene and found myself gazing around the room at the many friends and relatives who had come to pay tribute to my uncle. I could hear the whispered undercurrent of sounds in the room. My gaze stopped as I recognized my cousin Cindy standing behind the grand piano. Her belly protruded. She was about six months pregnant. Slowly I stopped breathing, squeezing the oxygen out of my lungs as I continued to study her. Why was the sight so familiar? She was wearing a maternity blouse. It was edged around her neckline in a soft cream-colored lace collar. The pattern was made up of a muted peach background, covered in fine chocolate dots. She was glowing. She was wearing one of my maternity blouses.

The recognition of this familiar garment left me dumb struck. *Was this a fluke or is that the blouse I wore just a month or two ago?* A wave of barely controllable emotion took hold of me. I found myself clenching my teeth. It was as if I had been bitten by a snake that was causing my body to retract into a kind of emotional paralysis. I was unable to breath. Unable to speak. I had no ability to react to my surroundings.

We stayed for an hour. I found myself avoiding eye contact or conversation with any of the guests. This was a time to acknowledge my uncle's passing, yet I was in my own head, struggling to deal with the image of my cousin in my maternity garb. I wandered over to where my mother sat in the corner of the living room not too far from my aunt, and between gritted teeth spoke quietly, with lips barely moving.

"Am I seeing cousin Cindy wearing my maternity blouse?"

She looked up at me with a puzzled expression. "Yes. I thought it was a generous thing to do. It costs a lot of money to buy maternity clothes. Besides, I didn't tell her they were yours!"

I continued to look at her and shook my head. *How could she be so oblivious to the potential impact on me? Her frugal upbringing could not allow her to give away these clothes to a stranger. Better a family member should benefit.*

Shortly after, we left the apartment with my brother and sister, driving in silence. I remained quiet, taking deep, prolonged breaths for the first five minutes in the car, trying to relieve the stress. The circumstances were beyond my control. *Just live with it. Let it go. She didn't do this to hurt me,* was all I could say to myself. But it still hurt, a kind of heavy weighty bruise to my psyche. The reminder was palpable and painful. I began to realize I could bury it all and function, but then just as easily have something like this blind-side me. It was something I couldn't share with anyone; something that was hidden, just below the surface, waiting to force its ugly head into my view, obstructing all else. My mother had no clue on the impact of her good will.

Chapter Fourteen
Beginnings and Endings

The day finally arrived to start college. It was March of 1965. I packed my belongings, hardly believing I was finally going to be out in the world again. I would be driving north past Newburgh where I had been hidden from the world to have my baby. Now I would finally reenter my life and live in a dormitory with two other girls on a State University campus in New Paltz, in the mountains north of the New York City. I always wanted to be a teacher and this school was known for its education program. Three main buildings of red brick appeared on the horizon, a beacon of hope, as we entered the town. These three-story buildings held the classes I would attend. There were also two large dormitories, across from the quad: one for girls and one for boys.

My dorm room in Gage Hall was one of a series lining the second-floor with polished linoleum and beige painted cinder block halls. It was spartan, with two bunk beds, three desks, and three slim chests of drawers squeezed into corners of the room, as well as slide-out storage boxes under each bunk. My roommates, Susan and Antonina (Toni for short), showed up just after I arrived and we tentatively smiled and said 'Hi' as we each said good-bye to our families.

As soon as our families were gone, I staked my claim.

"If you don't mind, I'd like to take the lower bunk away from the door. I'm a pretty light sleeper, so it helps to be away from noise and lights."

Toni quickly jumped at her chance to declare her needs. "That's okay with me. I'd prefer to be on a top bunk since I'm always cold and I'm hoping it's warmer on top." Susan was last to speak.

"I don't have a preference. I guess I can start out on the top of the other bunk, and if I change my mind, I can always move down since it looks like we don't have a fourth roommate."

She slowly moved to the other side of the room and began carefully unpacking some of her clothes into the slide out under the bunk.

I continued the getting-to-know-you ritual.

"I'm from south of here – Great Neck on Long Island. Where are you from?"

Toni was gathering her art pencils and piling them into a coffee mug on her desk. "Gee, we probably grew up about a half hour from each other! I'm from Lindenhurst, a suburb about thirty miles further east on Long Island! What about you Susan?"

"Um, well, I'm from upstate, about four hours north of here in a small city called Utica."

"I think I know where that is," I declared. "My sister Pat went to school in the area."

"Most people don't know much about it. It's only got a population of about twenty-nine thousand people living there. It's surrounded by lots of streams and mountains. It doesn't surprise me that most people are not familiar with it. Do either of your families hunt or fish?"

"Can't say that mine does. The only thing we hunt for is food from the A&P grocery store." I continued to fold my jeans into a neat stack to put in the dresser drawer.

"Yeah, same for my family. The Marone family grows some tomatoes in our backyard and the only hunting they do is for ripe ones from their garden for pasta sauce on the weekend."

Toni projected a wry impish smile, hoping we got her joke. She proceeded to reach up to stuff her underwear and t-shirts into one of the dresser drawers. The top of the dresser was at least three inches above her shoulders.

"Sounds like a nice place for a vacation if you're into that!"

"Yeah, lots of people come to the area during the summer to hunt and fish. My dad hates the summer because of all the tourists. He likes to fish and hunt, but not then. Says it gets too crazy and crowded with the flood of all those vacation types bringing their fishing waders and shotguns, all decked out in their hunting gear that they probably haven't worn since last year! He prefers the spring and fall. I kinda like it in the summer, 'cause I get to meet new people from outside of Utica. It's so boring the rest of the year."

"Hey, did you guys hear there's some kind of orientation this afternoon? Looks like our group starting this Spring is pretty small." I hung my skirts in the small closet.

"Yep, that's what I've been told," Susan responded.

Her thick black hair was blunt cut to her square jaw. Her ski jump nose made her look pert and all-American. "Don't 'cha wonder why everyone in our group is starting in March?"

She wore a dark blue paisley blouse with a Peter Pan collar and beige pearl buttons secured up to her neck, tucked into a matching dark blue pleated skirt that hung below the knee as if she was going to a church meeting, definitely not a Rolling Stones concert. There was something closed and sad about her I couldn't quite name.

"Yeah, I bet everyone has good reasons... Well, why don't we head down there together?"

Toni climbed the first two rungs of her bunk to reach for her purse. She was dressed in jeans and a lime green t-shirt with a beer logo. The curls of her cropped ember-colored hair bounced as she jumped back off the bunk ladder. She wore forest green and white plaid glasses that let the world know she dared to be different.

"What are you going to major in?" I asked both roommates, as we closed our dorm room door and headed down the hallway.

"I'm majoring in art. I think it would be too cool to figure a way to do something I love and make money at it!" Toni walked backwards down the hall as she addressed us. "How about you Susan?"

"I'm thinking of majoring in primary education. I've always loved babysitting and working with children." She turned her head away from us and seemed to suddenly be in a trance as she gazed away from us out to the dorm windows that lined the hallway.

"That's funny. I'm planning on majoring in education, but I'm not sure whether I'm interested in elementary or secondary grades. I've always gotten great grades in English, but I also love music. I sang with my friend Sandra in high school at different dances we had."

That seemed like a lifetime ago. Yes, I was always told I was good at using my language skills to explain things, even though the last year had proven to be inexplicable.

We headed over to the auditorium to attend the orientation for new students and hear about the policies of the school, when we'd get our schedules and who our mentors would be that would show us around the campus. We looked around and saw that we were a small group of about twenty-five students. At that moment, I knew Susan was right. We probably all did have a reason for starting late.

When the orientation ended, we headed back to our room along the path to Gage Hall to finish unpacking and get ready for dinner at the campus dining hall. Susan spread herself across her upper bunk, while Toni and I continued to put our things away. That's when I noticed something I couldn't ignore.

Toni reached down into her brown leather suitcase and took out a plastic prescription bottle containing black capsules, and placed it on her dresser. It was a strange moment when time stopped. The image of the bottle was eerily familiar. I realized I had been given a prescription quite similar after my daughter was born. I wasn't sure if Susan was sleeping or reading.

I whispered to Toni, "You're taking iron pills?"

I began to have a queasy feeling creep from my gut to my head as I saw the stared at the black capsules in the opaque pharmacy bottle. Toni bit her bottom lip.

"Yeah, I'm a little anemic. My doctor prescribed them."

Our eyes met across a chasm of knowing silence. Who would declare the reason first?

"Yeah, I took the same pills a few months ago, when I was anemic too."

We continued to look at each other, silently signaling while the truth percolated below the surface of our conversation. It was a turning point in our relationship. I knew I needed to tell her. The truth was going to burst from me if I didn't say something.

"I took them because I had a baby last December." I continued to stare at Toni, waiting to see a sign.

"A baby girl. That's why I'm starting school late."

The truth poured from my mouth like a river whose dam had burst. It was a total impulse and it felt good to speak the truth and be free of lies for the first time in almost a year.

"Are you shitting me? I did too…just two weeks ago. A girl too" Toni leaned back on the lower bunk, legs sprawled, leaning on her elbows.

We looked at each other in shock and disbelief: Could this be just a coincidence? The silence was thick as we absorbed what was happening.

"How did your parents react?"

Toni spoke softly.

"My freakin' boyfriend took off as soon as I told him I was pregnant. My family was supportive, and if I had wanted it, would have forced him to marry me, but I wasn't interested in a shotgun wedding with that jerk. They went into overdrive to keep it all hush-hush. You know the drill, I'm sure."

I looked over at Susan who was still stretched out across the opposite upper bunk on her side, her back to us, facing the wall. She had removed her flats and was very still, as if she were napping. I responded,

"You got that right! The last thing my mother would suggest was getting married. She was mostly concerned about keeping it a secret. But my boyfriend is still around. I told myself neither of us was ready to be parents, but the alternatives were totally awful. Did your parents ever volunteer to raise the baby?"

We spoke in hushed tones, assuming Susan was napping.

"Yeah. But realistically, they didn't want to raise a baby at their age and I couldn't see that happening. I was a good student in high school and they felt it would be better to keep it all a secret, let me have the baby and then start school. My mother made all kinds of phone calls and came up with a way to get me out of town so no one would know. My damn boyfriend high tailed it as soon as he found out, the S.O.B. If I ever see him again, all I would say is 'Eat Shit Faggot!'"

Her anger permeated the room. Susan suddenly propped herself up and looked at both of us. She had apparently been listening to our conversation prone, while reading her magazine. She tossed the magazine to the foot of her bunk.

"I guess all three of us are here for the same reason!"

She leaned over the bunk to look at us. Tears were welling up in her eyes, and beginning to drip down her perfect nose. Words began to stream out of her mouth as if they had been dammed up and had reached a tipping point.

"My son was born last November. My boyfriend wasn't interested in being involved either. He totally copped out; I was pretty much abandoned to figure it out on my own with my parents. They had been so proud of how well I did in high school. They made me feel like a failure. They were furious and they acted like I was the biggest sinner in the whole world."

She sniffed back her sadness, swallowed audibly as she swung her legs over the edge of the bunk.

"They didn't hide me, so I guess most people knew. I think it was their way of punishing me. I had been excited about starting college. I won a scholarship and was at the top of my class. And then, this happened. The whole town knew about it!"

"Wow." I collapsed on the lower bunk. I was dumbfounded by the coincidence of our colliding stories.

"Do you think the school knew about us? Is that why we ended up together? How weird. Do you think we are the only ones out of the group starting this spring?"

"I doubt it," Susan muttered. "So was it fate that brought us together?"

We sat in silence and looked at each other. Toni began to hum a familiar television theme.

"Is this a Rod Serling 'Twilight Zone' moment? Doo doo-doo-do, doo-doo-doo-doo. Cripes, do you think the school knows?" She twirled the curls hanging in front of her forehead through her fingers. It suddenly dawned on us that our group was unique.

Starting school in the spring was not typical. I thought, it couldn't just be us. I wondered how many of the other girls also had babies. And what about the boys? I suddenly remembered a conversation I had had recently with another student.

"You know, I was talking to one of the guys in our group named Paul who just started. He told me he was involved in a fatal car accident and his girlfriend was killed. He ended up in jail for the past two years, and is starting late because of it. I have a feeling everyone in our group has some kind of a story to tell."

Our unique bond based on the pain and loss of a child began our special friendship. We would go to class and come back to our room, close the door and confide in each other about our experiences and circumstances. As we went to classes, I often wondered what were the stories from our group yet to be revealed? I was still seeing my boyfriend; Toni and Susan had both been abandoned by the boys who had gotten them pregnant. One had given up a daughter, the other a son. What were the chances that we would be thrown together with so much in common? And yet, our experiences were very different, as we shared stories behind the closed doors of our dorm room.

"So how did your parents keep it a secret when they realized you were pregnant?" I asked Toni one evening when we both took a break from our homework.

"Well, they were very upset and worried about the family and neighbors finding out. My mother called all over the place and finally found the Salvation Army Home for Unwed Mothers. She explored whether I could go there. But they wouldn't take me until I was seven months pregnant, so I could only stay for the last two months," she quietly explained to us.

"What did you do for seven months?" Susan asked.

Toni leaned back on her desk chair and threw down her sketch pencil she had been using to complete an art homework assignment.

"I lived in my house, but was not allowed to be seen. If anyone came over, I had to go to the back bedroom and stay there until they left. I wasn't allowed to answer the phone or go out of the house. The Marones are a very traditional Italian family. It nearly killed my mother. You can imagine she didn't want to have to go to church to talk about it in the confessional! All my relatives and neighbors thought I was away at college."

"You mean you couldn't go outside or talk to anyone for the whole time? It sounds like a kind of prison."

"When I finally got dropped off at *Sally Ann* in New York City, (that's what we called the Home), it felt like relief. At least I could go outside. Occasionally, a small group of us girls got to go to the movies together or for a burger. As soon as I got there, they laid down their rules. No last names could be shared. Each girl had a roommate. We were told not talk about our background, last name, family, or anything personal. We were each given a wedding band to wear so when we went out of the building, we appeared married. Pretty weird, since if you saw a group of young pregnant girls together with rings on, you pretty much knew they were probably not married! Who did they think this was fooling?"

My jaw dropped. *I guess my mother had picked up some ideas about how to camouflage a teenage pregnancy with a wedding band.*

"What about you, Susan?" I asked. "How did your parents react?"

"Oh, pretty much the same way. I stayed home and stayed out of the way. It was hard to go anywhere without feeling everyone was whispering about me and staring. Especially since everyone knew who my boyfriend was and the jerk was obviously not around or involved."

Her voice was foggy as she gazed down and picked at her fingernails, avoiding eye contact with us. When she looked up, I could see her dark brown eyes were clouded, her brow furrowed. She had a look like the girl next door, but a demeanor of someone who had committed a crime.

We were all good students who were going to get back on track, carrying our individual burdens and emotional pain silently, without counsel except from each other. As the months unfolded, we immersed ourselves in our schoolwork, and tried to focus on the future. Susan pledged for a sorority. Toni started to hang out with a creative crowd from her art classes.

On weekends, we'd head down to the local college bar to drink cheap beer and dance on the twelve by ten dance floor to The Righteous Brothers' 'You've Lost that Loving Feeling', and Rolling Stones' 'Can't Get No Satisfaction'. I was a teenager again and gave myself permission to enjoy myself. Soon, I was getting asked out by boys from my school. It felt weird but exciting; having a boy show interest was great for my ego.

I'd go out on dates, and go as far as necking. I couldn't imagine being with anyone but Romolo.

Often, the boys would move on to someone new, once they realized I wouldn't give in. My heart was still tied to Romolo. By this time, his mother had returned to Italy for the second time, to address her latest maladies, taking his sisters out of school to join her. Later that year, his sister Maria sent me a letter to let me know they were in Italy, and asked me to write to her. I decided it was time to write back and tell her what had happened.

Dear Maria:

How wonderful to hear from you! How is everyone? Your mother? Your sister? School is wonderful and a great deal of hard work. I'm taking English, math, Africa and the Near East (a type of past and present day history course), music, and gym. It keeps me pretty busy with classes six days a week. The school system here is run differently than at other colleges. The entire year is divided into four equal ten-week quarters (the summer is one quarter). To graduate in four years, each student must take three quarters a year. Some take four, meaning they go to school all year long without a break and graduate in only three years. It's harder on this type of system: before the quarter has started it seems that mid-terms and finals are before you! Time goes quickly.

Concerning Romolo and I, yes, something has happened…something which I hope you and your mother can understand. Four months ago, I gave birth to a beautiful little girl. It was Romolo's and mine. I left my home last September and lived not far from this very college town until the time came. The decision to let her be adopted was Romolo's and mine. We felt very strongly that it wouldn't be fair to have our daughter grow up in an unhappy home, and that is exactly what our home would have been had we gotten married. It is very necessary that your brother get his education. Without it, he will never be able to survive in this fast-changing world. If I had married, I would not have been able to go to college, thus I would not be able to get any type of a decent job to help financially. Because of our decision, she will grow up in a happy home. The people who have adopted her love her very much, and I know I've made them very happy. I realize how wrong you must think our decision was, but if you stop and really think about it, I'm sure you will realize we made the proper and best decision.

Romolo and I plan on continuing to go to school and in four years or so, when I graduate, we will discuss marriage – if things remain as they are now.

Maria, all I can say about the past is that your brother is a wonderful person whom you should be proud of. What has happened is merely part of life: mistakes do happen, but when they do, if you learn by them, they are lessons in life. You won't make the same mistake twice.

As far as the picture goes, I hope you like this one. It was taken about two and a half months ago, after I came home…my hair has grown since then, but basically, I'm still the same old me!

How about sending me a picture of you? One of your sister too! Believe it or not, I miss you all. I can't wait to see you. I wonder who will travel to what country? You to America or me to Italy? We'll see…You'll probably win!

I just called Romolo. He said he got a letter from you telling him you hadn't heard from me yet. Did you really think I wouldn't write? Were you that busy last year that you couldn't answer my letter?

Well, it's getting quite late and I have a class tomorrow morning (Saturday). My mother, brother, sister, and grandmother are coming tomorrow to visit the campus. What fun!

Take care of yourself and please write soon! My love to you and yours,

Love,
Maxene

Who was I kidding? My letter was going to portray me as a totally in-charge young woman, using her head and not her heart to make decisions. I was hoping to convey that everything had been done the right way and the future looked bright. I always knew that below the surface of this façade, everything was definitely not all right. My heart still ached. But a stiff upper lip would be shown to the world and I was determined to move forward. Maybe eventually, I told myself, if I said it often enough, I would start believing what I was saying.

Romolo and I continued to stay in touch and see each other on breaks and occasionally during the school term. Neither of us talked about the baby we had given up, but focused on school and life in general. Spring flew by, as did the summer of 1965. Toni soon was getting serious with a young elementary teacher who had graduated from our college and now worked and lived off campus; she was spending more and more weekends away at her boyfriend's place, coming back in time for class Monday morning. She'd leave notes on whatever paper she could find. Sometimes, it would be toilet tissue. Other times it would be the back of a receipt or occasionally, a Playboy pinup.

"Hiya: I'm off for the weekend! Have a good one and see ya on Monday xoxo"

Susan had quickly met someone too who had a job and lived nearby. She attended class, but was struggling to keep up.

"I don't understand how I could be such a great student in high school and not doing well in college! This just doesn't make sense!" she complained. She was having a hard time applying herself. Instead of doing her work, she began to disappear to be with her boyfriend during the week and on weekends. The distraction was taking a toll on her grades and she was avoiding dealing with it.

Every few weeks, I would get on a bus and head into the city to secretly spend the weekend with Romolo in the apartment he shared with his two college roommates. Reflecting on the situation, I guess it never dawned on me that things could be different. I didn't even question the fact that I was making all the effort to travel to see him, and not vice versa. Was I more committed and in love than he was? I would never know. My roommates and I seemed to need a relationship to help us feel valued, to heal our wounds, and validate our existence. Some days it worked. Some days it didn't.

It was evening after a full day of classes, just before the Winter Break, and we were all in our room. Toni and I were finishing up homework at ten o'clock in the evening, sprawled on the two lower bunks, when Susan lowered her head and whispered,

"Did I tell you that today is my son's birthday?" Her voice quivered like a wounded bird. Her face revealed a pained expression; her unkempt hair sprouted in all directions, veiling her eyes. The dark circles under her puffy eyes gave the impression she hadn't slept, or she had been crying.

Toni and I stopped what we were doing, looked at each other and at her, unable to respond. We moved toward her on the opposite lower bunk and silently draped our arms around her shoulders, creating a warm human blanket. The three of us hugged, holding each other tightly in a circle of grief, silently acknowledging her loss.

"We know. We know. We understand... This is so hard." Toni tried to comfort her and held her tightly.

"I'm so tired, you guys. I think I'm going to bed," Susan declared sniffling back her tears. She climbed to her upper bunk and wrapped herself in the cocoon of her blankets.

An hour passed. Toni and I were still up, quietly discussing our plans and packing things for our break. Suddenly, we began to hear moaning from the upper bunk, where Susan was supposedly sleeping.

"I can't do it. No! Please don't! Why? Why? You don't understand!" We heard Susan muttering, crying, twisting, and turning in her bed. Perspiration began to bead on her forehead. She threw off her blanket and was thrashing about, turning from side to side. We both rushed to climb the bunk ladder and try to awaken her. She wouldn't respond. She began swinging her arms, her fists clenched like rocks, screaming and crying, panting, and sweating. Toni and I looked at each other in fear. We struggled to contain her, holding her arms down; afraid she would catapult off the bunk and injure herself.

"Susan, Susan, wake up! Everything's ok. Wake up!" Toni patted Susan's arm and brushed her hair back from her face, attempting to wake her up.

"Leave me alone! I won't! No! You can't! Don't!" She continued to sweat and thrash about.

"What the heck is she doing? Is she having a bad dream? She won't wake up! What do you think is happening?" I was beginning to panic, not sure what to do.

"I don't know, but I think we need to call someone!" Toni replied.

She quickly jumped down from the bunk and headed down the hall to find the Dorm Monitor, her electric blue terry robe flapping behind her.

"We think we have an emergency with our roommate!" Toni declared. "We thought she was having a bad dream. She's moaning, and tossing and turning in her bed and we can't wake her up. She's going nuts and we don't know what to do!"

"Go back to your room and make sure she doesn't hurt herself. I'll get help and be there in a minute!"

The dorm monitor called the campus doctor, who arrived within five minutes of the phone call and rushed down the hall to examine Susan. He found us still attempting to hold Susan down. "Can you wait outside please?" He took charge of the room.

We climbed down from the bunk and Toni turned to him to explain what we knew.

"A year ago today, her son was born, and was given up for adoption," Toni explained. "She told us that just before she went to bed."

"Thank you, girls. That is very important information. She may be having a nervous breakdown," the doctor responded. He opened his bag and searched for his hypodermic and a bottle of medicine.

"This should calm her down."

We paced outside our dorm room. After about an hour, we were allowed back in the room. Susan had been sedated. She was now calmly sitting at the edge of the lower bunk, head bowed, and holding on to the mattress as if she might fall over and crumble to the floor. We asked if we could help and were told to gather Susan's belongings and pack them into her suitcases.

It was a long night as we silently packed all of Susan's clothes and belongings, and waited for her parents to arrive. It felt like we were preparing for a funeral in slow motion, removing all remnants of her existence from our room. Toni and I gazed at her occasionally, as she sat in a medically induced fog, putting our arms around her to give her a silent squeeze to show her we understood her pain. Finally, at around four o'clock in the morning, the Browns arrived, having made the long drive from their home in the country to rescue their daughter and take her home. Susan never came back to school and we never heard anything further about her fate after that night.

Toni and I had been humbled by our roommate's breakdown and glad we did not have to deal with a replacement for Susan, once she had left. We often spent evenings talking about what we could have done to help her, but always came up dry of ideas.

"Why do you think this happened?" I asked one evening.

"She told me she desperately wanted to keep the baby and her parents wouldn't let her. They were very strict Catholics and she had sinned. I guess it got to her when it was the child's birthday. I think she was overwhelmed with grief."

"I feel so bad for her. She had been so successful in high school, and nothing seemed to work out for her once that happened. It makes me sad she couldn't turn it all around. But then, we know how hard it is..." I stared wistfully out the dorm window at the quad.

Somehow, Toni and I had gathered enough strength to cope and live through the trauma of our situation and were now working hard at being focused on our future. We had each other. Susan was emotionally destroyed by her experience and never could get beyond it. To this day, Toni and I talk about Susan and wondered how her life turned out. We never heard from her again.

Chapter Fifteen
Betrayal

It was finally Winter Break of 1966. I came home to my family; my first real break since starting school in early spring the year before. Now that I was home, I was feeling good, and glad I was to have time off. One day, when my mother and I were out shopping, we parked in a local mall parking lot. I was about to get out of the car, when she placed her hand on my arm to stop me from opening the door.

"I have something I want to tell you," she declared, eyes averted to the dashboard.

"What is it?" I innocently asked.

"I went in to the city so that Mr. B could give me a check, which was the last step of our agreement for the adoption. I have $1000 for you to spend as you wish. I think you should plan a nice vacation somewhere when you have your next school break."

I looked at her in disbelief. *The final payoff.* I thought. *Why does this man make me feel so cheap?*

"But when I went to his office, I noticed there was a new picture on his credenza. It was of a toddler, racing on all fours across the room. She had sandy hair and big blue eyes. I found myself drawn to it, wanting to look at it as much as I could. It looked just like you when you were that age..." She hesitated. "I think Mr.

B has arranged for the adoption of your daughter by his daughter and her husband. He may now be her grandfather."

All of me clenched into a knot, as we sat in silence in the parking lot, surrounded by Christmas and Hanukkah shoppers. There were no words possible at that moment.

Chapter Sixteen
College Years March 1966–1968 and Marriage

President Lyndon Johnson had launched Operation Rolling Thunder in 1965, the aerial bombing campaign that marked a critical turning point in the Vietnam War. It would mark America's first major offensive in the conflict. In the following two days, a contingent of Marines-America's first U.S. combat troops would land on the beaches near the U.S. air base at Da Nang. Johnson lamented:

"A man can fight if he can see daylight down the road somewhere. But there ain't no daylight in Vietnam. There's not a bit."

And yet, by the following month, President Johnson gave a speech that sounded like he was totally convinced of the righteousness of his decision.

"We have made a national pledge to help South Vietnam defend its independence. And I intend to keep that promise."

I knew boys from high school who had chosen not to go to college. They were quickly drafted and sent to the front lines. I breathed a quiet sigh of relief knowing that Romolo was safely ensconced in college for the next four years. Meanwhile, I was determined to get back on track, finish school with my class and turn my life into a success. I always enjoyed school and learning. Now I had the opportunity to be back in the community – no longer banished – with my peers. The war wasn't in my purview. I was a teenager again, but different from the rest. A ring was no longer necessary to protect me from prying questioners. Oh – but the stories! Luckily, my roommate and I had each other. On campus, Toni and I were constantly tested to keep our stories straight, but we managed. Without any grief counseling to deal with our loss, at least we had each other. It cemented the bond that would last decades and help us weather our hidden suffering.

The cloud of loss receded, but it was always there, looming. My daughter's first birthday came at a time when I was home for the Christmas break. None of my family ever mentioned it. It was as if it never happened. The weight of this event bore down on me. I spent the day pretending to study in my bedroom. My mother knocked on my closed door. "How are you doing? Are you feeling okay?"

"I'm okay. Just need to do some things for school and have some quiet time." Nothing was farther from my reality. I sat on my bed, reflecting on my experience of loss and consoling myself out of the gloom. *It was the right decision. She's got a family that can provide for her and hopefully love her. All I can do is try and make something of myself.*

Toni and I had each other to share our feelings, and our thoughts. Having given up her baby girl only two weeks before starting back to school, she dove into her work as an art major, but equally into her search for a new love in her life to replace her feeling of emptiness. We sat up many nights, after a day of classes and homework, for weeks after Susan had had her nervous breakdown, comparing our experiences and all the secrecy that surrounded them. I learned about her life at the Salvation Army Home for Unwed Mothers. She learned about my banishment to an apartment sixty miles out of town in Newburgh, New York. It was a much-needed outlet for both of us at a time when total silence about what we had experienced was the rule outside the walls of our dorm room. There was no empathy to be gained anywhere outside our friendship. Not even with our families. We both needed to stay focused on the future and move on.

Following our orientation to college, we were asked to take a physical education test to determine if we would be exempt or needed some remediation. Toni had been a star athlete in high school, winning many trophies. Now, only two weeks after having a child, she was required to take a fitness exam and failed miserably, never revealing her secret. Soon after, she was told she would be required to take a remedial physical education course, all the while, unwilling to reveal why she had done poorly. "It's just what I have do," she said philosophically one evening in our dorm room.

"Yeah, I know, but it's just not fair!" was all I could say.

In September, we were into our second quarter. I would often come back from class on a Friday to find a note left on my bed written on whatever form of paper my roommate could find before grabbing her things and rushing out the door.

Hey there! Off to spend time with Rob. Be back in time for class on Monday. Have a good weekend!

She had quickly gotten involved with Rob, who was a graduate of our college who taught elementary school. He wasn't much taller than she was and tended to take control whenever he could. She was off campus more than on campus. She was replacing her loss and sense of emptiness. After several months, everything changed.

"Looks like I'm pregnant. This time I'm keeping it. Rob and I have decided to get married so I'll be quitting school after the end of the semester and moving in with his family," she announced one evening in a matter-of-fact tone.

"Really?" my throat began to close. "I will miss you. You're very important to me. Friends forever, right? Promise we'll stay in touch?"

"Absolutely. You know I will! I feel the same way too. I guess I wasn't ready to be in school," she replied with a wistful look in her eye, her curly hair dangling in front of her eyes as if she was hiding from her new reality.

We hugged in silence, acknowledging our special bond. Her loss was too great. I was the only one of the original three roommates who would continue my education and graduate in 1968.

By the end of the next summer, I had made up for my missing months by going to school year-round. I was finally back on track with one less story to have to tell about where I had been at the beginning of my school career. The cloud, however, was always there, just below the surface, hidden by my good work ethic, my optimistic outlook, my social self and my drive. The self-talk helped with my head, but not with my heart.

Romolo and I continued to see each other. The invisible bond just wouldn't let us part. I would occasionally take the bus into the city on a weekend to stay with him at his apartment that he shared with two other roommates. The pull of our relationship was strong. While we were together, there seemed to be a code of silence about what had happened and an attempt to move forward. What was this bond? A permanent emotional cord tied us together...or was it imprisoning us? We never discussed it.

We continued to see each other throughout our college years and got engaged. I would often find myself in class staring at my engagement ring thinking about my future. He graduated a year before me and seemed unable to move forward by applying to schools immediately after graduation to pursue his medical degree and avoid the draft. Instead, he left the door open to the wishes of the U.S. government. He was drafted soon after graduation. He had no deferment excuses. The good news was he would be going through basic training and sent to Germany to utilize his pre-med biology skills in a lab on the base. The bad news was he was beginning to exhibit a passiveness and despondence I should have paid attention to. It was a sign of his state of mind that would later become a major issue. At least for now, he wasn't on the front lines of an unpopular war in Vietnam.

I graduated from college in three and a half years, proud to march and receive my diploma alongside my peers in 1968 with a secondary school teacher's certificate, majoring in English and minoring in education. I had accomplished my goal to graduate with my peers. I landed a job at the nearby town of Wappingers Falls as a ninth-grade English teacher starting in the fall of 1968. It was a good job, and I was excited to finally be totally independent. I lived in an apartment with a college graduate friend who was a new elementary school teacher; I bought a new car. I had a fiancé with a vision of marriage somewhere in my future. Things were looking good.

February of 1969, a huge snowstorm blew in right around my school's winter break. The sky was gray and cloudless, foreshadowing the pending storm. I had driven back to my parents' house for the week, anticipating Romolo would be coming home after completing basic training. The storm blew in with a vengeance. It dumped a four-foot-deep blanket of swirling, sticky wet snow on everything. Traffic came to a halt. Everyone was out with shovels, tunneling through their driveways, scraping car windows only to have the wind sweep across and cover everything with a new wet blanket. Kids made snow angels and formed hard missiles to be catapulted at each other. The laughter of children was muffled by the white silence that only happens when snow blankets everything. It was beautiful.

Due to the storm, Romolo couldn't travel south to report back to the Army for his last training session before being shipped overseas to Germany. He would have an extra week before he could return. He came over to visit soon after arriving back into town.

"Looks like I can't go anywhere until next week! I'm going to be shipping out soon, so I was wondering if we should get married now while I'm here? Then you could join me in Germany when you finish the school year. What do you think?"

I was stunned, excited, and scared.

"Are you sure? Well, of course yes, but we'll have to move quickly. School is out in June and I could join you then!"

My heart was beating fast. Would we finally get back on track and move forward together? I announced the decision that evening to my parents. My mother's response was not what I expected.

"Well, you might as well do it, since you two are determined. No point in me voicing an opinion. You'll find out once and for all whether it will work. Yes, do it."

Her voice was flat. She seemed resigned rather than elated. I don't remember my father voicing an opinion. That was pretty much par for the course back then.

We moved quickly to invite a handful of relatives and Romolo's parents. We ordered a cake, and I bought a white knee length silk and wool dress with small ruffles down the front. I was being practical: I'd be able to wear it again for other special occasions. Flowers were ordered and a justice of the peace in town agreed to do the service. A Chuppah, a canopy of white flowers was designed and placed in front of my parents' fireplace, under which we would be married, the one symbol of my Jewish heritage. It represented the home we would create together. We completed the ceremony by stepping on a wine glass to symbolize the fragility of life and our seemingly unbreakable commitment.

Chapter Seventeen
Germany

Shortly after our wedding, Romolo packed up and left for Karlsruhe, Germany, while I returned to my ninth-grade teaching job, still living in the two-bedroom apartment with my roommate, Dawn. Three and a half years after my daughter's birth, I had accomplished my goal; I had graduated from college, started my career as an English teacher and married my daughter's father. I was half way through my first year as a teacher in 1969. Birth control had been released to the marketplace in 1965, but only for married couples. I was now married and qualified to control my own fertility, even though my spouse was across an ocean on another continent, while I completed my first year as a teacher.

It was a fulfilling year. I invested my energy in creative projects for 'my kids'. Grammar and reading Shakespeare's *Romeo and Juliet* took on life. We built stage sets out of shoeboxes. We studied the era and planned a field trip into Manhattan to see the just recently released movie of the play. Seeing the excitement in the classroom was thrilling. Taking a trip into the city for many was a huge first time event. There was a buzz in the classroom as they assembled their stage sets and researched the clothes and furniture of the period. This was nothing like the dry and boring English class I recalled from my school years. The fact was, I was having as much fun as they were, and was determined to make this learning experience come alive and be memorable.

I had one class of honors English students. There were days when I would come home and would feel totally inadequate to teach these bright young teenagers; I was terrified they were smarter than I was. I would call home to talk about how things were going and express my concern about how to provide enough to these well-read students. My father offered me his simple advice:

"Just remember you get to read whatever you're assigning them the night before they get it, so you'll be fine." He had such a simple but memorable way of putting me at ease.

During this five-month period, between getting married and the move to Germany, my head and heart took over, continuing to work in separate universes. I was proving to be a successful, engaging teacher, while inside, I was anxiously anticipating being a wife to the man I had been involved with for ten years. I'd show up at class and find I had been scratching my arms due to a nervous itch, etching red lines like mini train tracks from my shoulders to my elbows. My students noticed and pointed out the marks.

"Have you got a cat attacking you?" My anxiety was showing up in strange ways, creating an itch that was driving me crazy even though on the surface, I appeared calm and in charge. I finally gave in and went to the doctor to see what I could do to stop this from happening. He prescribed Valium which I took cautiously during this period and stopped once. I wrapped up my year and started to pack my bags.

In June, once school was out, I joined Romolo in Karlsruhe, Germany, a town in the southern Black Forest area. I would need to learn how to live schizophrenically in two totally different cultures: the German and the American Army. I continued to educate myself and learn to cook and began to appreciate drinking German wine. Most importantly, I learned what it was like to be an American associated with the Army in Europe. This was a country still carrying guilt about World War II and was still playing host to the victorious Westerners. The old guard looked at us warily, not wanting to discuss what had happened during the war. The young people welcomed us and our culture; eager to adopt Western habits of clothes, music, and television. Within the Army there was yet another microcosm of two distinct cultures: those who signed up and saw their involvement as a career, and those (with whom we hung out) who were drafted and 'doing time'.

These draftees found refuge in losing themselves in the haze of marijuana nights, blurring their evenings with wine, music and food, hoping their stint would pass quickly and praying they didn't get reassigned to fight the war on the battle fields and swamps of Vietnam.

I quickly realized I couldn't sit around. I wanted to find work and contribute financially. As an Army spouse, I would not be considered for a full-time position with the American school on the base, since my husband could be moved to another post mid-year or transferred who knows where. I applied to the school on the Army base for part-time positions. I needed to do something with my time.

"Guess what? Even though they won't hire me full time, they are willing to consider me as a substitute teacher when full time teachers are out!" I announced excitedly to Romolo. It felt good to use my education, have a purpose and contribute while Romolo was working.

"They will call me a day in advance, and it sounds like even though my major was in English, it may be for all kinds of subjects, including math and boys' gym! This should be a riot!"

He seemed pleased that I had something to do.

Romolo did not want to be in the military and quickly found friends who felt the same. I began to recognize a haze that seemed to always be coloring his moods. Looking back, I think having to adjust to the American culture had taken a great deal of effort when he was younger. Now, we were having to adjust to the Army and the German culture. It was all too much. Most of his peers worked as lab technicians in the Army hospital on the base, and found any excuse to get together on off hours to commiserate. I became a great hostess as one of the only spouses among the crowd. I would dive into my *Joy of Cooking* or *Life Magazine* series of cookbooks from different country's cuisines. I learned how to whip up simple meals to fill these young men's bellies as their appetites grew with every toke. It was, of course, obligatory to learn to cook Italian and often would start from scratch, rolling out pasta dough, laying the freshly formed white strips out on cloth dish towels on my small kitchen floor to dry, as if I were drying edible laundry, and then dropping the pasta into boiling water to cook before stuffing them with ricotta and spinach and smothering them with my homemade pungent tomato, garlic, and basil sauce.

We lived 'on the economy' in a simple stucco apartment building on the sixth floor with no elevator. The apartment consisted of one small bedroom, an ample living room with a couch, two old stuffed gray chairs, and a tiny kitchen with a half-sized refrigerator and small stove. There was just enough room for two people to eat at a small drop-down half-moon table. When our Army friends would come to visit, the doorbell would ring and one of us would leap down six flights of stairs two at a time to unlock the door shouting, "I'm coming!" There was no lack of exercise, which enlarged our appetites for the evening's repast.

I adopted the European way of life, shopping for groceries with my basket over my arm, visiting the butcher and the baker, and the small grocer to buy fresh fruit and vegetables-just enough for my refrigerator which just reached my waist. It meant I shopped much more often, but I appreciated going to the bakery with its smell of warm, freshly-baked potato bread, crunchy on the outside and soft like butter on the inside, and seeing the bright crisp greens, warm yellows and vibrant reds of the vegetables that were fresh in the market. I learned to cook thick, white asparagus instead of the thin avocado-green ones we had at home. I rode my collapsible bicycle everywhere. I learned that regardless of my diminutive stature I needed to stand my ground when the larger German women pushed their way to the front of the line or through an aisle. Thrusting elbows out to my sides to protect my space and keep my position became a new defensive posture.

I was adapting to a totally different world. We took German classes in the evening from a teacher who had been a prisoner of war in the United States during World War II and had learned to speak English. Other evenings, we whiled away our time with Romolo's army buddies, listening to the Grateful Dead and Led Zeppelin, lifting our spirits, escaping from our daily reality, laughing, eating, smoking, and enjoying each other's company. These young men had been drafted and it had put a hold on their life plans.

There was Hawk, the eighteen-year-old red headed freckle faced soldier, a farmer's son who had graduated from high school and wasn't sure he wanted to be a farmer for the rest of his life, but hadn't quite figured out what he would do instead, when he got drafted.

Then there was Foxy, the 'older soldier' from Ohio, twenty-six years old with bright-blue eyes, a wry smile, thinning sandy hair and a handlebar mustache. He told stories of his many escapades and affairs with women back home. He had been painting houses and dreaming of being a writer when the Army called his number.

Paul, with the flame-red hair, was the young man who was known as 'The Red Baron'. He had started the underground newspaper, *The Armpit: All the News that Fits We Print.* It was full of stories of the conflicts and mishaps between the draftees and the 'Lifers' who were career soldiers and took their jobs very seriously.

We nicknamed the twenty-year-old from Texas, Rabbit, because he talked fast and moved fast. No sooner did Rabbit land in Germany than he had quickly gotten involved with a young German girl named Annaliese who worked in the Army PX. She had learned to speak English on the Army base and now had the unusual combination of an American Southern/German accent when speaking in English.

"Hey, y'all! Vas are vee going to do tonight? Venn are ya'll gonna pick me up, sveethartz?"

I learned much later after we were back in the States that Rabbit married Annaliese. Stories were told years later that once Rabbit's tour of duty was finished, he had carefully camouflaged some hash wrapped in plastic wrap covered in Vaseline on Annaliese's arm, covered it in a cast, and had her pretend it was broken as she stepped on to the plane heading to the States. No drug sniffing canine would ever find the stash which was just enough for private consumption. These were young men rebelling against their plights. Juvenile tricks could have cost them a great deal if ever caught.

There was one other married couple, Bret and Ellen from New England, who were living on the economy like us and adjusting to the different cultures. Somehow, the guys who were married never got coined with a nickname.

And lastly, there was Roger, an athletic twenty-one-year-old from Virginia who had dreams of becoming an Olympic athlete or at least a semi pro baseball player. He had just graduated from college with a physical education degree when he was drafted. He was the only one of our crew who was not working in the lab.

Instead, the army had assigned him to a missile site. There, he sat in an elevated watchtower for eight hours a day, in three and a half hour shifts, guarding the site.

Instead of being challenged physically and mentally, Roger was forced to sit by himself for hours each day, scanning the horizon. He snuck a transistor radio into the tower to keep his mind going. He even broke down and brought a book of crossword puzzles, something he hadn't done in years. Each evening after his watch, he headed for the gym to reenergize, get his body moving and rid himself of the state of extreme boredom that had enveloped him during the day.

Sometimes, he would show up at our place for one of our group gatherings where we'd pitch in for food, wine, and smoke. About two months into his tour of duty, we were sitting around staring at a candle burning on the coffee table, listening to Jimi Hendrix, full from our meal of Wiener schnitzel and spaetzli, when he declared his frustration.

"Hey guys, I don't know about you, but this assignment is driving me crazy. It's so bad I'm doing crossword puzzles to keep me going. I used to think it would be a breeze sitting staring at a missile all day! What a jerk I was! I'd rather be in the trenches fighting this war than sitting around like a mushroom. It's driving me bananas!"

Soon after that evening, Roger asked for a transfer and got his wish fulfilled. He was shipped off to Vietnam to the front lines of the war. The following month, the Army released the latest casualty statistics and names of the soldiers who had died in action in their newspaper, *The Stars and Stripes.* Ever since Roger had been transferred, our small group of misfits would scan the paper each month, hoping never to see his name. Then we did.

"Private Roger Bingham of Charleston, Virginia was killed in the line of duty, attempting to hold back the enemy from entering the town of Phuket."

We gathered together that evening at a local pub. We huddled in a back-corner booth to talk about Roger. Romolo took the news hard. "Damn! How can this happen? He was such a good guy. Physically in better shape than all of us. I'm blown away." Rabbit chimed in,

"Yeah, man, I can't believe it. I wish we could've convinced him to hang in there at the missile site. I know how hard it was, but this is worse."

Hawk sat silently, shaking his head and sighing, holding back tears. He had looked up to Roger as a role model of someone who took good care of himself, with a positive outlook on life. Foxy was sitting next to him and reached over and put his arm around his shoulders, and gave him a gentle squeeze of support.

"Yeah, this sucks big time. This goddam war has got to come to an end soon!"

We grieved that night and for months to come. We hung out together in a group effort to escape from the thought of a war looming large overseas. The threat cast a shadow over everyone; they could be reassigned to join the battle in Vietnam even as medics, and wind up like Roger. It darkened the cloud that was already forming over Romolo, making it even more difficult for him to enjoy simple pleasures. It was a powerful reminder of the impact of war and a somber reminder to be grateful we were in Europe and not Vietnam.

He and I often planned short trips over the weekend to get away from army life. Europe was very small compared to the United States. We drove to Paris in a day to visit his sister Maria who was attending the American School; we visited Amsterdam and toured Austria and Switzerland finding cheap places to stay or camp. We saved up vacation time and the first summer, spent a month in Rome, visiting with his friends, basking in a life style that started at ten in the morning for a light breakfast and continued when they took off from work between one o'clock and four to have a leisurely lunch, and relax on the piazzas or play tennis, before heading back to work a few more hours.

As the evening unfolded, the setting sun cast a golden glow on the many smooth white statues of bare breasted women, cherubs, and young virile men set in the many fountains anchoring each piazza. Dinner would begin around nine-thirty and continue into the night over multiple courses accompanied by pitchers of dry red wine as the traffic flowed around the piazza like bees in a hive. I could feel myself being lured into a life style that was totally different than anything I had ever experienced. It was unique and memorable as all my senses opened to new sights, smells, and sounds. By the end of my time in Italy, I was beginning to grasp meaning behind some conversations in Italian.

During that visit, we also traveled to Barete, Romolo's birthplace in the mountains, and visited some of his relatives. It helped me understand the huge change he had experienced. Once, he lived in a cement floored two-story stucco house overlooking the mountains, where the tallest and only ornate building in the town center was the church gleaming in gold foil, and multi-hued frescoes that were no doubt paid for by donations from the parishioners of the village who scratched the earth to grow vegetables and fruits and only had enough for a meagre existence...but the church needed to be beautiful. Everyone knew each other. I met his tiny wrinkled grandmother with her bright white hair pulled back in a bun and her leathery brown visage. She and I posed for a picture in front of his house, holding wheat sheaves in my arms with the warm Umbrian sun creating a glow around us. It was a magical trip that expanded my ever-widening view of the world.

Gas was only twenty-nine cents a gallon if we bought it on the Army base; travel was cheap. Five dollars secured a campsite, where we parked our used Volkswagen van. We had converted it with my homemade curtains flocked with red carnations on a white background and a bed made of a slab of foam rubber set on a makeshift plywood platform. We visited castles and small quaint villages, some of which camouflaged horrors, like Dachau, the concentration camp that was now a memorial; we saw bunkers and bombed out churches that had never been repaired. We were humbled...another graphic reminder of the impact and insanity of war.

Travel became a distraction from the day-to-day realities of the Army and yet at the same time, a sobering education. This was a two-year stint; within the first year, it became evident that most of these draftees walked around grudgingly biding their time. Their only respite was those evenings when we gathered to smoke, eat, and drink or traveled. The rest of the time, they felt imprisoned and resentful.

And yet, hope was on the rise. The Apollo 11, the first lunar landing by the United States was celebrated that year; we were excited and proud as we saw television reports that the 'Eagle Has Landed!' Television news reports also captured images of anti-war protests along with graphic pictures of American soldiers killed and injured. These reports were bringing home the instantaneous visual reality of war as no other war had ever done.

And at the same time, in the spring of 1969, in a farmer's field in upstate New York, a music festival like none other, called Woodstock was taking place. We watched clips on the news about the war, the lunar landing, and the festival. It was a media circus of events and bloodshed, of music and wailing, of celebration and rebellion. While the American public was elated by the success of lunar exploration, they were growing weary of a war they felt we couldn't win. These soldiers, even though they were drafted, knew they would not be coming back to cheering crowds if they made it through their time.

***

Lieutenant Mayhall was a 'lifer' who oversaw the lab. His shirts were always neatly pressed. His slacks had a sharp crease down the front. His Army regulation boots were shined every morning. He was a man whose whole career was the Army. He took his job seriously, and had no patience for these draftees who only wanted to do their time and get back to their lives. He often called them up for minor infractions and they were slowly losing patience with having to obey him.

During one of our evenings hanging out together, the topic of the lieutenant and his demands came up in conversation.

"Ya know, I'd like to put it to the lieutenant. He is on my case all the time, and I've just about had it!" Foxy had been reprimanded numerous times for unpolished shoes or not buttoning the top button of his lab coat. His voice expressed his frustration.

"You are so right! We oughta stop him in his tracks so he realizes he's a jerk. What if we took out the spark plugs from his car?" Hawk was getting excited about the potential prank.

"I got a better idea. What if we dumped sugar into his gas tank? That would stop him in his tracks for sure! Give him a sense of how it feels to have your life stop." Rabbit jumped up from the couch to address the group.

"Okay, I'm in. We just need to make sure to do it when no one's around and get rid of any trace of evidence." Foxy couldn't hide his excitement.

Romolo bought the five-pound bag of sugar the next day. During a break the following morning, while the lieutenant was in his office with the door closed, Rabbit and Foxy found the lieutenant's car in the base parking lot outside of the lab. Hawk stood guard to make sure no one saw them. They carefully lifted the hood, and funneled the sugar into his gas tank, using the base newspaper, and got rid of the empty bag and the makeshift funnel in a nearby dumpster.

At lunchtime, the Lieutenant announced he would be going out for lunch and would be back in an hour. He grabbed his coat, put on his cap, and exited the lab to meet some officers at the Officer's Mess Hall. He unlocked the car and threw his coat and cap on the back seat. He inserted his key in the ignition and listened as the engine groaned as if its belly was infected with a virus. He jumped out of the car, slamming the door behind him and marched back to the lab in a fury, his eyes nearly popping out from behind his wire rimmed glasses. The veins on his temple were bulging.

"I know some of you guys have messed up my car!" he shouted in a loud voice. "I will find out who did this and will be taking action against the perpetrators!" He stormed out of the lab.

The draftees smirked at each other in silent satisfaction.

"We'll probably have hell to pay, but it was worth it!" Foxy chuckled.

Although Lieutenant Mayhall couldn't prove who had done the deed, he decided to take action against Romolo and Rabbit whom he believed were the culprits and asked for their transfer to another hospital. Romolo along with Rabbit received the news. They would be transferred to another base farther north in Germany. This childish prank caused disruption in friendships, housing arrangements, and jobs. It meant I could no longer substitute at the school on the base and would have to look for a new place for us to live and a new job.

We received the news that we were transferred to the main base in Heidelberg as of the following month. I began the search for an apartment, seven kilometers north in a small hamlet called Leimen. Since Romolo was finishing up at the old job and needed our car, a black soldier, Sergeant Wilson, from the old base, volunteered to drive me around to look for an apartment. This was 1970 when civil rights were still being fought for in the U.S. There still were states where interracial dating or marriage was against the law. One of the few places that appeared to be accepting of differences was the army. We were in a cocoon of acceptance. I learned quickly that this acceptance was still to be fought for on the 'outside'.

If the sergeant accompanied me, we got strange looks from potential landlords and a less than welcoming reception to apply for their apartment. I soon realized that if I inquired about vacancies alone, explaining that my husband was yet to be transferred, I had a better chance of securing a place. I had to ask Sergeant Wilson to stay in the car at the curb.

"It's okay missy. I understand. Ah'm from Georgia so it's not unusual to me."

It made me sad and puzzled to think the world was that biased. Eventually, I found a simple place on the side of a hill on the same street as a beautiful local brewery with its enormous copper beer vats gleaming through its front windows. We moved in the following week and began again to adjust to a new place. The apartment was a two-story walk-up. I soon found a job at the bank on the army base and learned to count money in U.S. dollars and Deutsche marks. This was not my chosen path, but long ago, I had learned that the path is never straight. Survival required flexibility and an optimistic belief that you can overcome most challenges. Every time there was a twist in the road, I could hear my father's favorite saying from St. Jerome: *"Good, better, best. Never let it rest. When your good is better, make your better best!"*

Chapter Eighteen
Oh Canada

We were nearing the end of Romolo's two-year assignment in Germany. I flew home first, while he finished his tour of duty over the next month.

"I guess I'll be going back to my parents' home to wait for you? We'll have to figure out where we go from there."

"Yeah, I guess so. I'm not sure what that will look like, but we'll see…" was all he could say.

We were both returning to the U.S. with no job, no home, no furniture, just our wedding gifts stored at my parents' house and our clothes. Upon his arrival, Romolo showed up at my parent's house, greeted everyone, and suggested we go out for a coffee. We went to a small local diner, where the coffee was hot and the food was home cooked. We asked for a quiet booth in a secluded corner of the place and ordered coffee and a piece of homemade apple pie in celebration of being back in America.

The entire diner sparkled with stainless steel walls and ceiling; lemon yellow and magenta neon signs advertised beer and homemade food. It was a surreal environment for us after sitting in German biers tubes with their rustic wooden walls, mugs of deep amber beer, hand carved signs, and hearty meals of bratwurst and sauerkraut. This was our first 'date' back in the U.S. as we tried to reconnect and figure out our future. The conversation was not what I had expected.

"I need some space to sort things out. I'm not comfortable staying at your parents' place. For now, I think I should stay at my parent's home which is very small, and you stay at your parents' until we decide what we're doing."

I was in shock. The cold steel walls and bright signs around me receded into the background of my consciousness. The tinkle of beverages being served and the soft buzz of patron conversations became white noise. The adjustment to the American culture, figuring out a direction in our careers and the health of our marriage were all on the line.

Why can't we pick ourselves up now that we're back and move forward together? I feel the burden is mine to always be the cheerleader, the one with the energy and ideas despite my own reservations.

"If you need to, okay. But this needs to be a very temporary arrangement. We're going to have to figure out where we go from here."

The arrangement was less than ideal. We were a married couple of two years staying at our respective families' homes while we attempted to figure out the rest of our lives. Within a few weeks of his arrival, he announced, "My brother Ennio is going to California to explore opportunities. I think I will go with him to see what it is like. I'll be back soon."

"Are you sure? Do you think that there may be opportunities?" I was not invited and was on my own.

"Yeah, Ennio has been telling me things are booming on the West Coast."

I had my doubts, but tried to stay optimistic. I stayed at my parents, trying to avoid their questions and focused on finding a job to keep me busy and with resources to function.

"So Romolo doesn't want to stay here?" My mother had a sixth sense about things and could tell all was not well.

"Um, he's trying to adjust after two years in the Army and wanted a little space. Now he's telling me he is going to explore California with his brother. Who knows? Maybe we'll be moving out there." I tried to sound optimistic but I knew my mother was seeing through it.

One way or the other, I needed to be out on my own as soon as possible. I found an administrative job at a local publishing house to tide me over, while I explored being able to land a full-time teaching position for the following year. I discovered that the teaching profession had begun to shrink in the early '70s as the Baby Boomers had pushed through the school system like sextuplets moving through the birth canal, leaving vacant classrooms and too many teachers anywhere near a metropolitan area. If I wanted to be a teacher, it was shaping up that I would need to go to a more remote location to land a job. However, I was married and expecting this to be a joint decision, not just mine; I held off doing anything until Romolo returned.

Within a few weeks, he arrived home with his brother. The trip was a distraction which hadn't changed his reality. We still had no home and he had no job.

"So how was California? Did you identify any opportunities while you were there?"

"Nah, not really. Nice place but very expensive. I realized I needed to come back, even though it was a nice break after the Army."

It was as if his reality was only his: it didn't seem to include me. I got the distinct feeling that I was by his side, but he was myopically looking at the world only in front of him, without seeing me by his side as part of the picture.

On one of our many camping trips to get away from the Army base, we had traveled to Spain, along the Costa Brava. There, we befriended a Canadian couple from Toronto who were on vacation that summer at the same campground. Peter was an engineer. Jennifer worked as a dental technician.

"You guys should come to visit. Toronto is a great cosmopolitan city. It's the New York of Canada! I would bet with your degrees, you could land a job there, no problem!" Peter seemed keen to promote his city to us.

They seemed nice and told us excitedly about the multicultural environment and the growth of the city which was bringing significant opportunities where the U.S. dollar could buy a great deal more and we could afford to start our lives as civilians. Both of us felt like nomads: no home base, not relating to the politics of our own country as the Vietnam War was winding down. Shortly after our return to the States, I had received a letter from the Peter and Jennifer. "Hey, remember that nice couple we met camping in Spain? They've written to us!"

I was excited to hear from them.

"Yeah, they were great people. What do they have to say?" Romolo's posture straightened up with interest.

"They're inviting us to visit them and be their guests so we can explore opportunities in Toronto. What do you think? It would be kind of interesting to see Canada." I was hoping this would be a way to bring us together. We still had a feeling of flexibility and wanderlust to continue exploring where we would settle, most probably away from our families. The idea of getting in the car and driving to another country was a familiar experience for us.

We decided to make the trek and explore our next possible home. It was like getting in the car on a Saturday morning in Karlsruhe, Germany, to explore Austria or France from our home base. Within ten hours, we could be in another country where they spoke our language and had multicolored money, just like in Europe. They even had red bullet streetcars, like Germany. We could feel at home there.

I quit my administrative job and we headed north. Both of us felt like strangers in our own country after living abroad for two years. With our college degrees, and youth, the Canadian immigration system welcomed us and easily awarded us 'Landed Immigrant' status, the equivalent of the U.S. green card. The country was growing and hungry for self-sufficient professionals who could contribute to their economy. We discovered that Toronto felt very much like Europe with its clanging streetcars and diverse population. We thought we should look at the possibilities that might be there for us.

When I graduated from college in 1968 with my teaching certificate and bachelor's degree, there was an automatic requirement in New York that graduates had to gain a master's degree within five years of graduation or lose their teacher's credentials. It was one way the government could sort out who was serious about being a teacher and who was doing it simply to avoid the draft. I was determined not to lose my certificate, hoping that my education would be useful as a teacher somewhere. I applied to the University of Toronto Graduate School and took the graduate entrance exam. Within a month of my application, I received an acceptance with an award for an assistantship to help finance my way. I was ecstatic.

"I received an offer to go to graduate school with a scholarship! Unbelievable!" Something positive was happening because of my hard work. I had a purpose and could proactively take charge of my situation. I now had a plan for the next year.

"That's very good. I'm happy for you." His monotone voice did not match his words. I could have been telling him I bought milk and bread. He was expressionless.

He spent his days at our friend's place doing nothing. His wavy hair grew long, a statement of his anti-establishment mood. He sat watching television, unshaven. He mumbled his answers when I tried to engage him in a conversation. He looked truly morose and without a direction.

"What are you going to do?" I asked one evening. "I'm going to stay now that I have been accepted into graduate school. You know it's important to me. You could find work if you wanted to."

"I'm glad this has happened for you. I just don't know what I want to do. I studied science so I could get into medical school. Then I got drafted. Now, I'm just not sure anymore."

For the better part of the next month, he continued in his malaise, whiling away his time in indecision. Then one evening, I felt compelled to raise the subject again.

"I'm not seeing you make any effort to do anything about work, but we can't stay here with our friends much longer. We will need to find a place soon. I need to understand what's going on with you. You need to find a job so we can afford it."

Our eyes met. I could tell that he was about to announce something important as he pursed his lips and shifted his position on the couch.

"I don't think I want to stay here. You have something you are committed to. I don't. Maybe I should go back to my parents' place until I figure it out."

I was blindsided by his answer. I never expected he would give up that easily and could feel my anger, seething below the surface. I tensed as I reacted to his announcement. My fists and teeth clenched involuntarily.

"Well, if that is what you want to do, then do it!"

I was frustrated with his inability to decide and show commitment to me. I was now mirroring what my mother had said to me when I told her we wanted to get married. I knew I preferred that he not be there reminding me daily of his lack of energy, focus, or direction. I had survived so much and had no tolerance for his inaction. The following week, he packed his bags.

"I hope you do figure it out. We have our whole life in front of us. I finally caught a break and I'm grabbing it. I hope you find yours."

"I hope so too."

It was all he could say as he gave me a peck on the cheek, picked up his suitcase, and headed for the door to a waiting taxi. I inhaled deeply as the door clicked shut. The familiar numbness in my soul took over and as I slumped down into the living room couch, I felt like a part of me had died, and yet I knew there was a new beginning waiting. It was a flaccid ending to our passion that had lasted ten years. It was the end of our marriage, but not the end of our relationship, as I would find out many years later.

Chapter Nineteen
Land of Sunshine and Hell

I had learned so many years before that when faced with adversity, focus on the future and work hard. I took on my graduate studies as if I had a job, an all-consuming full-time activity. Many of the teachers who were employed and doing their graduate classes at night alongside of me, glared every time I asked a question, as if I might be prolonging the evening by my enthusiastic involvement. They were there to get credits that would impact their rate of pay. I was there to learn.

I found a house to share with four roommates to keep my expenses low. Peter, an American draft dodger and want-to-be writer had a job with a local tabloid. Joanna was a young woman who was studying to be a dancer. John and Elsa were a couple who were starting out in their relationship and worked in retail. And then, there was me: the only full-time graduate student who was going it alone in a foreign country without family as back up. I had determined I needed to make my way independently and would no longer rely on my parents to help me solve my problems. It would be hard, but I was determined.

In June of 1974, I completed my Masters of Education. My goal was to pursue work related to my major in English. I landed my first job at my housemate Peter's tabloid employer, a Canadian rag that you could buy at the checkout counter next to the *National Enquirer* at most grocery stores. The paper was full of rewritten stories from other tabloids from around the world: mostly sensationalized bizarre tales with lots of distorted pictures of weirdos and freaks and impossible feats of nature with headlines that screamed at the reader: *"My Child Was Born with Twelve Fingers and an Eye in the Middle of His Cheek!"* I would often ride the streetcar and see local workers avidly reading the paper from front to back. A little escapism went a long way to ease the routine of their daily lives.

After I landed the job, I moved out of the shared accommodation into a studio apartment down the street from the paper. I answered calls at the front desk, wrote a help column using the byline "Just ask Mary", and sent out inflatable naked full-sized female dolls that were advertised in the paper to attract lonely male readers, including those in the prison system. Occasionally, I was asked to translate and rewrite German tabloid stories utilizing my rudimentary German. I was starting from the bottom of the ladder in a job that didn't take advantage of all my sacrifice and hard work. It was a paycheck desperately needed to get back on track.

I tried applying to school boards for a teaching position. I was told I didn't have high school grade thirteen, which in the Canadian system was normal before starting college. But I had an undergraduate degree, a teacher's certificate, a year under my belt as a ninth-grade English teacher, and had just completed a master's degree in one of their universities. It became evident being American would work to my disadvantage in securing a teaching position in Canada.

By this time, the Vietnam War had caused fifty thousand war resisters to make their way to Canada. These young people left behind friends and family and headed to Toronto, Montreal, Calgary, and Vancouver. They would need to blend in and find work. However, it would not be easy. Canadians were going to prefer their own first. Even with my graduate degree, I was told I could be hired and rated only as a lower level teacher with less salary if there were any positions open, but there weren't. The reality was that in the early seventies, Canada would prefer to hire Canadians, even though my papers entitled me to work there. I was an American who would not easily get into the system. I was discouraged from bothering.

I developed a network while in graduate school and decided to pursue other avenues. I was asked to get involved with a group of fellow graduate students in a research contract studying the impact of adult television on school-aged children for the Canadian Radio Television Commission, a federally funded government organization not unlike the FCC. I jumped at the opportunity to be paid and get into something more challenging and aligned with my interests. It led to a second-year part-time contract, and finally, one of the graduate professors informed us there were a couple of openings for contractors to help the provincial educational television station, *TVOntario*, deliver workshops to teach students how to use portable television technology as a learning tool in the classroom. I had struck career gold! This was my ticket to a new career outside of the education system, and yet still in education.

I was now employed five days a week, half of the time doing the research and the other half sharing a contract with a fellow graduate student, running workshops with school aged students, helping them to learn how to use the first portable video recorders as well as a mini studio to make short programs in order to apply their writing skills to create scripts, edit their work, adding voice over and music, and learn how to work as a team. We were mentored by the creator of the workshop and soon had the expertise to deliver high-quality sessions to roughly two thousand students per year.

These were wonderful days full of feeling valued, seeing the light in children's eyes as they transformed an idea into a creation for all to see. I would start my day playing James Taylor's 'You've Got a Friend' which set a mood of optimism as I hummed the lyrics and lifted my spirits. I had come to a place of peace within me. I was on my own, successful in my work life. I thought I could survive anything and had the strength and will power to rely on myself. I felt as if I had become my own best friend. Taylor's lyrics were a perfect way to start my day.

Within a year, I scraped together a deposit and could rent an apartment in a house in a better part of town. I had reestablished myself as a single person with a stable income and a few friends. One day, as I sat on the front porch, my neighbor, a Japanese-Canadian woman named Mika, invited me over to meet some of her friends. It was my first venture into meeting people socially. Simon was sitting on her porch and greeted me. That was the innocent beginning of my descent into hell.

He was a tall, dark haired Englishman from Manchester, who had come to Canada when he was an adolescent. He always wore a cap over his ear-length black hair. I was mesmerized by his good looks, English accent and brilliant mind. He was so different from Romolo in personality. He was expressive while Romolo was an introvert. He showered me with attention. I guess I fell under his spell.

He collected books. He sculpted imaginary beings or everyday people he observed on the street. He wrote. He captured the world in his work, but seemed to always be on the sidelines, observing rather than participating. As a young teenager, his family emigrated from Manchester by sea. His father had been a dashing, intense young man with the same dark hair and eyes, as Simon, but a much shorter stature from what I had been told. He was known to flirt with any attractive female that passed him by, even if his wife was by his side. He was a chef on a merchant ship and hoped to ply his trade in Canada.

As I got to know his mum, I learned more that would later help me understand Simon's attitudes and behavior with women. She told me how her husband often denigrated her in front of her two sons. Within five years of arriving in Canada, he began an affair with a woman he met in a local bar, and the verbal attacks increased at home. She told me how this behavior made her feel less and less adequate. She sought help, while her husband declared he was leaving to live with his new lady friend.

They divorced shortly after and mum was now responsible for going it alone in Canada with her two sons. Simon was sixteen and his brother Mitchel was thirteen. Witnessing the breakdown of their parent's relationship and their father's abuse of their mother left an indelible bruise on both the boys' psyches.

While still in high school, Simon ended up almost dying from peritonitis and was operated on and hospitalized for a lengthy period. This left him frail and outside of the high school social system. He never graduated and soon after, left his mother's home, setting out for California to explore screen-writing opportunities. After three months doing odd jobs, he returned to Toronto broke and was hired by a local taxi company. He figured he could study people from the driver's seat while he made some money, and work on his sculptures and scripts at night.

Both boys had lived for years witnessing their father degrade their mother. It helped them form a distorted view of relationships and women. Mitchel experimented with drugs, trying to escape the pain of his father's abandonment. By the time he was nineteen, he had overdosed on LSD while at a friend's, and, thinking he could fly, jumped off the fourth-floor balcony, almost killing himself and landing in a hospital with multiple broken bones. Mitchel was a gifted artist who could never get his life together after the accident. After recovering from this near-death disaster, he left Canada to return to England, where a local religious cult took him in and converted him into a follower. He landed a job at the post office and handed most of his paycheck to the leader of the group.

He wrote preachy letters to mum letting her know he was now saved. They typically said things like:

I am at peace. You could be too if you understood the Maharishi's teachings. See the light! Stop your mortal sinning and join me in a better way. I can save you as I have saved myself.

Your Loving Son

Letters like this would come once every few weeks. Mum would read them and weep. She had lost her son and could no longer communicate with him unless she became one of his converts. Reality was no longer possible in his world. Her other son, Simon, was driving taxis and occasionally visiting with her. He too revealed a dark side that she did not understand.

His piercing Charles Manson brown eyes could look through you. He let all his fares know he was driving taxi temporarily; he was a writer and an artist. He had a strange camel like gait, hunching forward as he walked. His ear length coal black hair peaked out beyond his cap.

As I got to know him, I realized he was a brilliant, disturbing, creative person. His previous illness during high school had changed his life. He focused on his health and exercised regularly. He was a powerful presence of six foot one. I soon learned that while he sculpted beautiful one of a kind pieces, he often destroyed his work upon completion. He showered me with attention wanting to be together all the time. He was definitive in his personality. It was exhilarating to be with someone who appeared upbeat and in charge, intelligent and attractive after having suffered for so many years with an introverted man who carried his depression around him like a dark cloud over everything.

My judgement was misguided by all his attention. I had spent the last few years catering to Romolo's depression, leaving very little for me emotionally. It seemed to be all about him. After a few months, Simon moved into my apartment, and everything began to change. His attention mutated into jealousy over the slightest things. One day when I had just returned from hitting a tennis ball against a nearby school wall, he began his inquisition.

"Where have you been for the last three hours?" His queried in his crisp Manchester English accent.

"I was practicing my tennis swing against the handball court at the high school down the street." I could feel the hairs on the back of my neck standing up. It felt like an eight-year-old being questioned by a parent.

"Sure, you did. Who were you meeting there? You just go there to meet guys, don't you?"

"No! Not at all. I didn't meet anyone and just practiced by myself!"

He grabbed my racket from my hands as his rage began to percolate. He raised the racket above his head with a threatening gesture toward me.

"Come on now, tell me the truth!"

"I told you: I just went to practice!"

In one powerful motion, Simon slammed the racket against the kitchen table, breaking the head from the neck. All I could think of at that moment was it could have been my head separating from my neck. I stood in silent disbelief, shaking to my core. Strings sprung from the head of the racket as if trying to escape from his fury.

"You won't need to practice anymore."

This was the beginning of my descent to a place I did not know. What could I do to assure him of my commitment? How could I fail in another relationship? What was wrong with me? If only I could show my sincere commitment, maybe then he'd stop being jealous! Would I ever have a decent caring partner in my life?

Over the ensuing months as I rode the subway to work, I would find myself staring across the aisle at all the commuters. They all looked confident and focused on their day. I gazed into their eyes believing they couldn't possibly see me. They gazed back and I quickly looked away. It felt like they were looking through me. I had no presence. The old numbness that had helped me to cope with other trauma in my life returned. I let my hair grow long. I stopped wearing makeup and avoided looking at mirrors. I was once again in coping mode, somehow believing I must deserve this and unable to advance or retreat. I became invisible. Powerless and invisible.

Until I showed up at work. There, it was as if a switch was flipped and my inner self emerged, able to function and interact. It was now my safe-haven. At home, I was determined to make it better. I saw Simon's artwork and knew he had potential to do great things. If only I could help him see it, perhaps then his confidence in me would rise and we would be happy together. We did manage days and weeks of peace, but no sooner did I feel comfortable and at peace than his jealousy would rear its head like a serpent about to strike.

He began to be more physical, finding the slightest excuse to push me around or slam me into a wall. He thought it was fun to keep me off guard. There were times when I arrived home at dusk after a busy day at work, and none of the lights would work. He had busied himself during the day and unscrewed all the lightbulbs. On another occasion, I went out shopping and came back to my car to find I had four flat tires. He had released the air while I was in the store. He was slowly and steadily eroding my sense of self, my stability, and my ability to even feel I had control over a light switch. Off balance.

I was twenty-nine. Early on, I had told Simon about my daughter and he appeared empathetic. He shared with me that he had a son by a first marriage whom he saw occasionally. Now, after an unusually long period of relative peace between us, he suggested we should have a child since I was approaching thirty. I acquiesced; he had hit a cord with me. It was a desperate attempt to recreate what I had lost and maybe help to prove my commitment to extinguish his rage. Foolish, foolish thought.

Shortly after, I became pregnant. I told no one, not even my parents. I just wanted to make this work and announce it when I was ready. Into the second month, I began to bleed and my doctor ordered an ultrasound. He called me into his office to tell me the news.

"Unfortunately, it looks like you've miscarried and lost the embryo."

I reacted immediately.

"I don't think so. I still feel pregnant," I insisted.

He called for another pregnancy test, and when it came back positive, he sloughed it off.

"You probably still have high hormone levels which will subside over time. We should go ahead and schedule a D & C (a dilation and curettage procedure) to remove any remaining fetal tissue."

How could I argue with the doctor? I booked myself in to the hospital to have the procedure. I still felt pregnant. After settling into my room, the doctor came to visit. I once again expressed my doubts about having lost the baby, but he insisted: he believed I had miscarried, but due to my insistence, he decided to order one more ultrasound that evening.

The next morning, just before I was to be wheeled into surgery, the doctor returned with the results. I was indeed still pregnant! Apparently, the fetus was tucked way back in my tipped uterus and had not been seen before! He prepared the papers to release me.

"What would have happened if I didn't insist that I was still pregnant?" I had to hear his answer.

"Oh, if we had gone ahead with the procedure, I probably wouldn't have told you what I had found."

I was shocked. It was my first introduction to not assuming everyone else had answers. It was time for me to trust my own judgement. By the third month of my pregnancy, the hemorrhaging stopped. I realized this was the same thing that had happened to me when I was seventeen, but back then, I didn't know anything.

Ben was born in 1977, six weeks prematurely and weighing just under six pounds. That short period in the hospital felt like a vacation away from the stress of the relationship and all responsibilities. My focus was totally on seeing my baby who was in the preemie nursery. In my usual efficient way, I'd leave notes on my bed in case of visitors.

"If I'm not here, you can find me visiting the nursery!"

I should have known things would not change with Simon. He made few visits to the hospital after the baby was born. When he did, he began to mutter that the child didn't look like him. It didn't matter. Ben's arrival changed my life. I was no longer invisible because of him.

Shortly after Ben's arrival, Simon and I quickly married on the courthouse steps. My parents were informed about all of this after the fact; it was one way I kept them out of my life and business during this period. I was totally and completely in love with my child. I was experiencing what I had missed. I often found myself gazing at him as he slept, reflecting on my life. His tiny head fit in the palm of my hand. His lashes were long like my daughter's. His silky cap of hair was dark like Simon's. His demands as a preemie were significant.

For his first three weeks, he remained in the hospital while he gained enough weight to be brought home. I traveled to the hospital daily to breast feed him and bring the extra bottles of milk which I pumped at home to leave with the nurses and give him every conceivable advantage. During this period, my pediatrician was on vacation and a replacement doctor who looked like he was ready to retire, asked me what I was feeding the baby. When I said I was pumping at home and breast feeding my baby at the hospital, he shook his head and said, "Why don't you just go ahead and buy formula, given he's a preemie, to ensure he feeds well?"

I had already read about the benefits of breastfeeding, even if it took more effort. There was no way I was giving up on this no matter what! While I was feeding antibodies to Ben, I was experiencing the full bonding experience that I would not have missed for the world. This was yet another moment in time where I finally stood my ground. I learned that a preemie eats less but more often than full term babies, and once I came home, I was up with him every three hours, nursing and rocking.

The Canadian health system allowed me to stay home for seventeen weeks with the equivalent of unemployment insurance checks helping us survive without my paycheck. After four months of being at home, I needed to return to work; I qualified for subsidized daycare. I started a journal about Ben's development, observing the slightest changes with wonder. His first birthday passed and after a slow start, he began to catch up quickly, learning to crawl, walk, and speak within months. I was in awe of everything he did. I wrote in celebration:

Journal Entry – *November 1978:*

Ben is crawling and trying to walk! And in just a short month or so, he has begun to name many things: our cat Tasha, our dog Choo, the words bird, bear, diaper, and rabbit. All sort of half-stated with either the middle or ending left trailing. But oh how he practices and wants to communicate!

After having spent four months of intense mother-son bonding, it was a bittersweet experience to deliver Ben to daycare. We needed the money and I had no choice. Soon after, Simon's badgering and jealousy resurfaced.

"You sure this is my kid? I'm thinking it might be the guy next door."

"Absolutely not! Look at him. Ben looks more like you than me, his hair color, even down to his feet!"

As the badgering continued, and his rage became more intense over the slightest things, he continued to imply that I had a problem. "I think you've got psychological problems. You need to get counseling. I can't seem to help you."

He was slowly chipping away at what was remaining of my emotional confidence. The difference now, was I had another human being, one whom I loved unconditionally. One whom I was determined to protect. One who gave me my purpose and my sense of self. I would not become invisible again. I was desperate to find help, any kind of help. Ben was almost eighteen months. I talked to my pediatrician who recommended a psychiatrist and I made an appointment. My journal took on a new subject:

Journal Entry – *January 4, 1979:*

I am beginning therapy to organize my thoughts and my life. To see what is and is not. I state this here in case anything should go wrong. My son means so much to me that I'm beginning to gain strength. I only want to keep him away from harm to his body and his soul. He is so precious and has so much positive potential. This must not be tainted or misguided. Nothing will stop us from accomplishing happiness and eventually harmony dear son. You deserve it too much...

Dr. Rosenthal, a dark haired matronly psychiatrist with small Ben Franklin glasses, met me in her office, a well-appointed comfortable place to talk, consisting of two pale blue wingback chairs facing each other and a side table next to each chair. Mine had a box of tissues on it. There was a *Life Magazine* on the coffee table between us with a front cover displaying a picture of the actress, Jane Fonda, known as 'Hanoi Jane'. She was smiling as she perched on an anti-aircraft North Vietnamese gun, not far from the POW camp known as the 'Hanoi Hilton' where American soldiers were being subjected to all manner of torture. Even though the war was winding down, veterans and soldiers alike called her a traitor and had no love for her anti-American activities supporting the Viet Cong. It reminded me of why I was still in Canada after being in Germany and experiencing the Army as a draftee's wife. I was totally apolitical and wanted nothing to do with war. Besides, I had my own war to fight.

The doctor had me complete a questionnaire prior to the first meeting. She had informed me when I made the appointment that she only takes on clients with whom she feels she can help in six to ten weeks, rather than providing on going counseling for years. As I sat across from her, I quietly tried to explain that I just couldn't seem to 'get it right'. She asked questions and listened intently.

"I hear you. So exactly what's going on at home?" She peered over her glasses studying me.

Within three meetings, she began to get a picture of what I was dealing with at home and what the real issues were. Tears flowed. Stress was released. I had a safe-haven.

"I'm not suggesting you leave him, but for the sake of your child and you, you need to know there is a safe place to go if things get bad. I would like you to do the research to know where you would go. There are safe houses for women and children leaving abusive situations. Please consider it."

"Okay. I just feel like such a failure! I feel like it's my fault somehow!"

"Actually, you're not. You're incredibly strong. You've been through a lot and you're feeling vulnerable with good reason. Take care of yourself and your child. That is what is important right now."

A week later, over the weekend, while Simon was out driving his cab, I finally called a safe house.

"Women's Habitat, can I help you?"

"Hello? I'm calling because my doctor suggested it. I may need to use your place to get away from my husband. I need to know what I need to do in case of an emergency."

"Yes, of course. We take in mothers and children when they are in danger from spouses who abuse them. Is that your situation?"

"Uh, yes, it is." I was finally labeling my experience.

"I can put your name on our waiting list. If the time comes when you need help, call and we will give you the address and directions so you can find us. One thing we insist though: under no circumstance do you share this information with your husband or anyone else. Understood?"

"Yes, I understand," I answered in a muffled voice, hardly believing I was hearing these instructions.

"How many children do you have?"

"Just one. My son is a year and a half." It was an automatic response after all these years, but there was always a little voice in my head telling me that this was not true; I had two children.

"Okay. Just call us and we will help provide room, board and counseling for up to six weeks. Do you work?"

"Yes. And Ben goes to daycare that is subsidized."

"Great. If you need tokens for the streetcar or subway, we can help with that too."

"Thank you." Now, I officially had an exit strategy thanks to Dr. Rosenthal. My early childhood dream of witches and giants was now a reality. I would know how to flee the giant and save Ben!

I soon realized things were not going to change. I had bruises that I hid. I had a black eye that I told colleagues was caused by a fall, after he slammed my head against the refrigerator. Wearing sunglasses to work was a dead giveaway. My government research project had ended and I had landed a contract doing research for the television station to test programs, along with my workshop contract. Simon had begun to be very uncomfortable with the fact that I had taken his advice and sought counseling, while I continued to thrive at work. He was beginning to see me getting stronger and fighting back both mentally and physically.

I had been seeing Dr. Rosenthal for about a month. One afternoon, I was working in my office at the television station which I shared with another contractor doing work at my desk on a project, when Simon showed up with Ben in tow. He had taken him out of daycare and traveled to my office with him…the one place where I was successful and had control. He knew it was the last horizon of my waning identity.

"Here, I brought your son to you. I know how much you want to be with him."

He placed the eighteen-month old on the floor with his diaper bag and with a smirk, quickly exited the office, saying, "I'm going to have to leave now. Good luck."

There I was, Ben on the floor innocently looking up at me and all my colleagues staring and whispering about what had just happened. I had to act quickly. I quickly grabbed my coat, Ben and his diaper bag, totally embarrassed as I exited the office.

I wandered the city streets, knowing that to return to our apartment meant a confrontation, something I did not want to do. I wasted the next number of hours, bought a coffee and a small container of milk for Ben and two donuts, and sat with Ben on a park bench near the city hall, thinking about what to do. I knew at some point I had to go home. Finally, around dinnertime, we took the streetcar back to our one bedroom apartment. The baby needed changing and food. I was physically and emotionally exhausted. I entered the apartment and found Simon pacing in the living room.

"So where have you been all day with my son?"

"Walking around the city. I did not want to come home to a fight." I placed the baby on the changing table and grabbed a clean diaper. Once he was changed, I grabbed a teething biscuit to hold his appetite over, while I prepared his dinner, fed him, and placed him in his crib, which was squeezed into a corner of our bedroom.

"Well I don't believe for a minute that this is what you did. Who were you seeing?"

"No one. I just told you I walked around the city." His eyes grew large and his face began to turn the color of rage I had seen many times before.

By this time, we were standing in the living room and with one lunge forward, he swung at me with an open hand across my face. I slammed backwards into a freestanding wooden bookcase, causing books to fly off the shelves like birds being startled by a sudden loud noise and flapping and fleeing from a tree, and in turn, the whole bookcase came tumbling forward, hitting the back of my head as it crashed to the floor and knocked me over. I pulled myself up and headed to the bedroom. I grabbed Ben, and ran out the side door, not exactly sure what I would do next. I was in full survival flight mode.

I ran down the street, hair flying in all directions, Ben perched on my hip. He began to cry, sensing the danger. A half a block away, a police car was coming down the street. I stood in the middle of the street, waving my free arm to call the car to my attention. The officer stopped in front of me and rolled down his window.

"Yes ma'am. What is happening? Do you need help?"

"Yes officer. My husband is going crazy and I just want to go back and get my things and leave with my baby."

Little did I realize that a blue and purple lump had begun to form on my right cheek, just below my eye, a graphic sign of how dangerous the situation had become. I felt no pain, just a sense of urgency to remove Ben from potential harm. I had mustered a kind of heroic strength that surprised me. No tears. Just energy directed at protecting Ben and removing us from harm.

"Okay, get in and I'll drive you home."

We entered the apartment through the front door. The officer glanced into the living room and saw the war zone of scattered books and the broken book case strewn across the carpet. Simon was in the kitchen, calmly pacing as he stirred a mug of tea.

"Hello Officer. I see my wife has brought you here. Did she tell you she's under psychiatric care?" He appeared relaxed and self-assured.

"Okay, thanks for telling me. Your wife wants to get her things and leave. I would like you to stay in the kitchen with me while she gets her things, okay?"

"Of course, no problem."

I rushed into the bedroom, not sure what to grab, perching Ben on my right hip, fearing to let him go. I found an old suitcase in the closet and lifted the laundry basket full of dirty baby clothes, dumping its contents into the suitcase. I grabbed some essential toiletries from the bathroom, grabbed a few things out of the closet and from the dresser and checked to make sure I had my wallet, checkbook and credit cards. The whole exercise took less than five minutes. This would have to do. We exited the apartment with the officer carrying the suitcase.

"Where would you like to go?"

"I'd like to go to my girlfriend's house for now, if you don't mind driving me."

"No problem. Just give me the address."

We drove across the city and I was dropped off at my girlfriend Lila's apartment. In the early days of my relationship with Simon, he had introduced me to her. They had met at a poetry reading in town and he had invited her back to our apartment for drinks. We became fast friends and I learned about her dog sitting business which she did on the side, while she worked for the telephone company and dreamed of running her business full time. She was a stout woman of Russian descent with an earthy sense of self. She kept her long blonde hair pulled back and neatly tied in a ponytail. She wore no makeup and had strong cheekbones and lively hazel eyes, but dressed in baggy comfortable clothes that would not attract male attention. From the little she had revealed to me, I got the impression she may have had trauma with men in her life, and decided it wasn't worth exploring any more. For her, her two Borzois and one Sheep Dog were her companions, her children and her life. Taking care of others' animals fulfilled her. Her clients loved her caring, loving way with their pets and she had built up an entirely separate life from her job at the telephone company. It kept her extremely busy seven days a week.

She lived across from the racetrack with her dogs in a walk-up apartment over a store. She had come to Canada via New York and had a few family members who lived in the suburbs. From the little she told me, life was very hard in Russia and she was determined to make a life for herself in Canada. She soon confided in me that she always wondered why Simon spoke so negatively about me when I wasn't around. She seemed to have a sixth sense about the dynamics of our relationship.

"Now that I have met you, I realize Simon seems to have the problem. You are a strong person and I think he is trying to break you down!"

Lila's place became my temporary haven. On the second day, Simon showed up and started banging on the door to Lila's apartment.

"Let me in. I know you're in there. I'm your husband. You have my son. Lila, she needs to come back now!"

"Sorry Simon, she doesn't want to come back and I won't force her. Why don't you just leave and let things cool off or I will be forced to call the police!" Lila was my guardian angel.

It took several hours of this back and forth before he finally stopped his ranting and left. That evening I let Lila know I had an alternative place to go.

"I don't want you to feel threatened by him. I can't stay here and have that happen. I'm going to call the women's place I've already talked to."

I called the number which I had kept in my wallet, and the counselor confirmed there was a room available the next day. She gave me the address, reminded me to promise to be careful not to share the address, especially not with my husband. After a sleepless second night, Lila drove me and Ben to a simple white clapboard house in a working man's subdivision on the outskirts of Toronto. There were no signs to let you know it was anything other than a family home. The yard was fenced with high metal fencing. I rang the doorbell and was greeted by the counselor who invited me in and quickly secured the double locks on the door. Soon I was filling out a questionnaire about my circumstances. It was a surreal moment to be once again hidden from harm in a secret place. But this time I had chosen it, and it felt right.

Journal Entry – March 23, 1979:
The deed is done. One violent outburst too many. Bruises and fear. Police and anger. Ben and I are out of the house and safe at Women's Habitat. A noisy, children-packed place where the thermostat gets put up to 30 degrees Celsius to keep the Jamaicans warm and Ben is loved by all their kids. Reason and patience no longer prevail. But a great deal of support exists and we'll make it just because of love.

Over the next few weeks, I learned the rules of the house. Some days I was on clean up duty after dinner, doing dishes, moving fluorescent orange plastic stackable chairs on top of long stark white plastic tables so that I could wash dining area floors. On other days, I helped in the kitchen, preparing cheap meals consisting of large quantities of frozen vegetables, a little meat, and lots of potatoes, or macaroni and cheese. There was always ice cream for the children. I soon realized I was one of the lucky ones. I had a job and daycare. Many of the women at the house were totally dependent upon their abusive spouses and had attempted to leave many times, only to go back because of their economic dependency. In the peace and quiet of a room I shared with Ben, I had time to write again in my journal:

Journal Entry – March 28, 1979:
It is one of the amazing things about people: they adapt; they survive! Ben and I have now been here four

whole days and a routine has almost begun. And the stories to tell! Mothers of three to six children with no jobs, no homes, no skills, and nowhere to go. And the humiliation for years which finally ended in violence. Only one woman has been fortunate enough to be without children and only three months married before the brutality started and she fled. Good for her!

All these images and stories of these days will be recorded to reflect on later. Right now, there is only energy for surviving and getting through yet another day…

I had escaped and left the car behind. I was finally paying attention to my own survival, the voices inside my head that could differentiate from what I knew was healthy, and what my gut told me was undeserved. I was given free tokens (since my car was with Simon) to take the streetcar and buses to travel to the daycare and to work. They provided practical advice about how to move forward. I could stay there for the next six weeks to get my life back on track.

Journal Entry – March 30, 1979:

Almost a full week here. Everyone is in their rooms and I sit in the echoing dining room. Orange plastic chairs stacked so high that I can't see the top…so that I could wash the floor. Refrigerators humming with franks and hamburgers, and drink crystals in bins on the counter to make pink and yellow liquids under the guise of juice.

It is quiet. Upstairs, little boys and girls sleep, while mothers wrestle with the reality of busy, peaceful loneliness.

Soon, I gained the courage to call Simon and demand that he return the car, which was in my name, or suffer the possibility he would be accused of theft.

"I'll give you the car; just tell me where you are."

"No I can't do that. I've got a restraining order against you, so just stay away from me. Don't try to come to my job. Just leave the car down the street from our apartment unlocked, with the keys under the mat and I'll come and get it. Please don't be there, or I will be forced to call the police. I mean it!"

"You're making a huge mistake. We can get counseling and solve our problems."

"Not right now. Just leave the car so I can get our son to daycare and go to work."

A day later, after work, Lila picked me up and we drove to pick up the car, all the while, scanning the streets in front of us and the rearview mirror, expecting Simon to suddenly appear. I quickly retrieved the keys from under the mat as we had agreed, said thank you to Lila, and drove around the city for forty minutes, making sure Simon was not following me. The glow of the city sparkled and shed light on my regained freedom. I found my way to the daycare, greeted Ben and held him close for a full minute, my face nestled against his neck, smelling his baby smell as he gurgled and giggled his greeting. I placed him in his car seat and headed back to the safe house. It was one more step for me to gain back control and never let it go again.

Chapter Twenty
Draper Street

The adjustment had been gradual. Living in the safe house was like stepping into another world after having my own place (even though it was a tumultuous one). Sharing one small bedroom with Ben in an unassuming suburban house with mothers and children changed my reality. All of us had one thing in common: we were in hiding. Black, Hispanic, poor, middle class; it didn't matter. The great equalizer was a controlling out of control spouse who posed a real threat. For some, this was going to be merely a break from the stress; they would eventually go back, rationalizing that they had no ability to fend for themselves. Dependency would reign, even though it was an unhealthy environment with danger always lurking. But not for me. No way. Not ever.

Six weeks at the safe house had flown by in a blur. Simon could not find me, and I was at peace with my decision. Every weekday, I got up early, took Ben to daycare and went to work, not discussing my situation with anyone. And now, it was time to leave and make it on my own somewhere. I contacted Lila in preparation for my exit. Her apartment building was being renovated into high-end condos that she could not afford and she was going to need to move.

She and I had talked about sharing a house somewhere in town. We took a weekend, scouring the city for affordable housing and found an old Victorian townhouse, not too far from the Globe & Mail, Canada's national newspaper. It was a semi-industrial area, with aging turn of the century worker's homes that stood proudly after almost one hundred years; their brick painted chili pepper red, now peeling like sun burned skin, with sharp peaked roofs trimmed with broken white gingerbread. Some were beginning to be gentrified by new owners. Others, like ours, were being rented out in their current state.

It was a grand house with twelve-foot ceilings and large rooms. The kitchen could accommodate a full-sized dining table and chairs. Cream-colored painted cabinets covered two complete walls with a door onto a postage stamp unloved backyard overgrown with weeds next to an empty lot with more of the same. The house was in reasonable shape, except, as we found out later, when we dropped anything on the floors. The living room had an uncanny slope toward the street; if you dropped or spilled anything, it would roll quickly toward the front of the house. Ben was walking by this time, and he quickly learned to lean forward as he left the living room to walk from the front of the house toward the kitchen.

A tall flight of stairs led to four bedrooms and a bathroom that we shared. I quickly got to work decorating Ben's room with wallpaper displaying dancing monkeys wearing bright orange shorts swinging among tree limbs sprouting lacy green leaves, in hopes he would find the move into his own room pleasant and inviting.

We settled in: Lila and her two Borzois, (her Sheep Dog had died), Ben, and me. With one extra bedroom, we decided to find a roommate to cover some expenses. Through someone Lila knew, we found Barbara, a stubby woman with wire-rimmed glasses and a heavy smoker's cough who preferred t-shirts and jeans to skirts or suits. A quirky, creative soul, she was a good twenty years older than us. We invited her to join our household.

Barbara was a bright divorcee who wrote freelance articles for magazines and newspapers. She took her smokes outside onto the porch and had a nip or two every day. We learned she had other issues we were not aware of. Every other week, she went to the local psychiatric hospital for counseling.

"So, how's your counseling going, Barb?" I queried over dinner one evening.

"It's okay, I guess. It's better than being locked up in the hospital, for sure! I've done that already once. I'm not going back. I just need to remember to take my meds so I even out a bit more. It's not a problem."

I must have looked surprised as I reacted to what she had just told me. "So, your medication helps you? What happens if you don't take it?" I was afraid to hear the answer.

"Well, I sorta get a little haywire. My ex-husband used to complain that I'd go off doing crazy stuff in the middle of the night, eh? I'd be like that for, I dunno, maybe a week or two, sometimes three or four, having a great time and being very productive with my writing, and then something would happen, and I'd sorta crash and not want to do anything but stay in bed, eh? It messed up our relationship, even though I know he still loves me."

Barb was bipolar, and the meds helped her. We hadn't seen any of that extreme behavior so far; we were satisfied she was managing it well. Lila knew her ex-husband (I never knew exactly how); he had been the one to refer her to us as a roommate. Unfortunately, she had already moved in when he told Lila about her past transgressions while they were married. He was very open about how difficult it was to handle her when she was manic, throwing parties, and staying up all night, only to become depressed a few days later and refuse to eat, work or come out of the bedroom to see the light of day. He told us that she quite enjoyed the manic state and didn't like having to temper it with the meds. Too bad we didn't know this before she moved in. We did notice that she had a peculiar smell about her which we later realized was the alcohol permeating through her skin.

The first few months in the house on Draper Street were uneventful as we settled in to our new routines. Ben loved running around the large kitchen, and occasionally squeezing himself inside one of the lower cabinets that contained all our plastic containers. He'd put one of the larger plastic bowls on his head like a hat, and with a wooden spoon, would proceed to bang on the remaining containers, amusing himself with the percussive sounds he could create. It was wonderful to see him playing with such a free spirit. Sometimes, as I would head out for work, I would find stubbed out cigarette butts on the front porch, or scattered pieces of ripped up family photos, letting me know that Simon had discovered where we lived and was now stalking us.

There was an in-town little pocket park down the street that had children's swings, slides, and a play scape as well as a flower lawn and some benches for parents or guardians to watch as their children played. On weekends, when the sky beamed bright blue and the sun shed a golden light, the weather beckoned to take Ben outside. On these occasions, I'd walk down the street with him holding hands to the park so that he could take in the glorious sunshine and play outside. After all, this was Canada, and we knew that once the weather turned, we'd be inside for the better part of six months or bundled up transforming us into robots in our movements as we played in the snow.

On occasion, Simon would suddenly appear on our street in the taxi he drove, reminding me he was figuring out our routine. I could never predict his behavior. If we happened to be walking to the park when he came down our street, he'd slow down in his taxi, roll down his window, and silently follow us with a sneer on his face, a cigarillo hanging from his mouth. Ben would look at him, with a confused recognition on his young face. Simon did not stop or acknowledge him. He just kept driving at five miles an hour, following us. I looked straight ahead, heart pounding in my chest, refusing to acknowledge his presence and quickened our pace. Once we entered the park, he would drive away.

On another occasion, I found my red Honda Civic had been moved at an angle from its parking spot on the street, its back end sticking awkwardly out into the road. Only a very strong person could lift the back bumper and move the car. I suspected who it was. There were also cryptic notes left on my car.

"You're finally coming out of the closet. I'm glad you're enjoying your new life style as a lesbian with your girlfriend." To all of this, I remained calm but angry, silent but seething at this man who would not leave me alone.

Meanwhile, Lila and I noticed clear empty bottles of a product with a white label with 'Alcool,' the generic brand of alcohol sold by the retail outlets, written on it. They were piling up daily in our recycling bin. We figured out they were from the government-controlled liquor store and were their cheap pure drinking alcohol. Our roommate Barbara was consuming one or two of these bottles a day, surreptitiously mixed with orange juice so she didn't look like she was drinking. Her behavior was becoming erratic and we were starting to get concerned. One Saturday morning, after a walk to the park with Lila and her dogs, Lila, Ben and I returned to house to discover Barbara in the kitchen.

"Hey girls, how're ya doing? Howz my liddle buddy? I know I said I'd cook dindin tonight, but I didn't make it to the groschereee store, so d'ya mind switching wid me?"

Barbara was sprawled on her elbows across the kitchen table. She lifted her head, to greet us, her papers spread all over. It was only ten o'clock on a Saturday morning. She sat in front of a tall glass of orange juice. It was not a breakfast drink. The familiar alcohol smell was present.

"I guess so. What are you drinking, Barbara? It's only ten o'clock in the morning!" I was not happy finding her in this state.

173

"Oh…jus some juice and a liddle nip to start my day. I'm getting some good writing done…"

She leaned back in her chair, trying to control her wobbling head. We kept our conversation brief. All three of us quickly exited the kitchen not sure what to do next.

A week later, on a Sunday morning, while my roommates were out, I was getting dressed in my bedroom, when Ben slipped out of his crib and wandered into our shared bathroom. Barbara's open pill bottle was tipped over on the sink and a few bright blue tablets had spilled out onto the edge. Ben had grabbed them and was sitting on the bathroom floor, playing with them when I walked into the bathroom.

"Ben, what are you doing?"

"Candy?" He innocently held up a pill toward me, implying he was asking permission to pop it into his mouth.

He looked up at me smiling and wide eyed. I gasped.

"No Ben! Put that down right now! They are not candy; they are bad for you!"

I bent down, scooped him up with my right arm, gathered the loose pills and dropped them into the open pill bottle with my free hand, and placed the cap on the bottle, twisting it shut with my teeth. I marched into Barbara's room with Ben under my arm and threw the bottle onto her bed, slamming the bedroom door behind me. I was shaking uncontrollably. I had just avoided a disaster.

After Ben was in bed, Lila and I discussed the situation at the kitchen table in hushed tones. I explained what had happened.

"I can't trust Barbara as a roommate. She has only been here three months...but her drinking and lack of care with her medications. It's just too risky. I can't take a chance that Ben will find her meds again, only the next time, I'll be rushing him to the emergency room to have his little stomach pumped. No way."

"I agree with you totally. Sorry about this. I had no idea she was that bad when I invited her to live here. Yeah, we need to tell her it's not working."

The next morning, we asked Barbara to leave. Lila and I approached her as she prepared her breakfast. I cleared my throat, took a deep breath, and kept my message simple without getting into details.

"Barbara, Lila and I have decided not to have a third roommate. So, we're giving you notice for the end of the month."

"Seriously? I thought this arrangement was working out well. I guess I messed up leaving my pills around?"

"You sure did. Ben almost started eating them thinking they were candy. We just think it would be better if you leave."

She didn't argue. She called her ex-husband and arranged to stay at his house until she could figure some other form of accommodation. He cared for her enough to help; he just couldn't live with her anymore and we now understood why.

We kept our word and didn't try to find another roommate. Lila and I decided we could manage. Life once again settled down into a routine. No more stalking from Simon and no one in the house I couldn't trust. It started to feel almost normal after traveling a long harrowing road. I was once again eliminating threats to my existence and learning how to declare my needs and fend for myself.

During that first year as a single mother, I found myself simply wanting to cocoon with Ben, do my job, and heal. I didn't need to date or complicate my life. I knuckled under and focused on work and being a good mother. I continued to take Ben to his periodic checkups with my pediatrician, Dr. Lewis. He was the doctor who had referred me to Dr. Rosenthal, the psychiatrist who was instrumental in helping me see the reality of my life with Simon. Dr. Lewis was a tall, curly-haired young physician with a warm personality, and an easy manner with children and parents. He could see that I was beginning to blossom as I took charge of my life. One day, after giving Ben his booster shot, he asked me,

"Are you taking care of yourself? Are you getting out at all? You seem like a smart woman who deserves to be able to date occasionally."

I looked at him and smiled.

"Yes, I suppose so. But you know, Dr. Lewis, there are a lot of turkeys out there. I guess it only takes one to change my mind. I'm not in any rush, thanks!"

The world was full of sunshine after the hell I had been through. I wanted to keep it that way.

I began to consider how I could end up with a job back in the States to be closer to family. Perhaps, in my most secret and wildest of dreams, I could make myself available on the off chance my daughter came looking for me. It going to require some serious job searching from a distance. For the time being, at least I had subsidized daycare to help me manage. Long term, I knew I would head South at some point. It was a question of how and when yet to be determined.

Chapter Twenty-One
Taking Back Control

Being a single mother in another country with no one to depend on but myself was the best management training I ever had. I learned to manage finances and time, prioritize tasks, complete projects, and juggle multiple responsibilities. I needed to be coach and counsel, financial manager, major convener of fun, dishwasher, laundry maid, cook, cleaner, and nurturer. While I loved every minute of it, there were days when I was overwhelmed. I was in control of my life and Ben's. But sometimes, the energy output was greater than my capacity. On those days, I would collapse from exhaustion after putting Ben to bed. I would spend my day hearing about employee issues and problems and providing counsel, and yet I had no one to understand my issues and challenges. My mother often would ask how things were going and whether I would settle down and remarry or was I just going to be career woman? I always answered the same way: "We'll just have to wait and see. My career is important, and Ben and I need the money. I'm in no hurry!"

No matter. Ben filled me up every day watching his growth and development. I blossomed at work as I learned more and more about my capabilities which were constantly challenged.

After several years doing contract work, I had landed a full-time manager's role at *TVOntario*, a publicly funded television station. I was responsible for developing and delivering management and employee training, dealing with employee relations, establishing a recruitment function, and representing the station on the Ontario Provincial Government's Affirmative Action Council. I had staff and people who depended upon me. I had truly found my calling and relished in my ability to challenge the status quo and learn something new every day. There is no doubt my life experiences made me resilient.

Gene, my boss, was a nervous executive with bright white hair and a marshmallow face. He relied on confident, competent staff to get him through the day. He stood six feet tall, but operated as someone who wore his vulnerability on his sleeve, worried about the impact of the slightest challenge in his role as Vice President Human Resources, formerly Personnel.

Occasionally, I would get asked by Gene to present information about our department's results to the Board of the organization, even though he was the executive and my boss. He knew his limitations. Whenever Gene was asked to speak in front of groups, his nervousness would surface and he'd shove his hands into his pockets; this way he wouldn't visibly fidget. His fingers would scurry around the coins that were inevitably in his pockets, causing his change to jangle and chink, creating a distraction for the audience. If he helped himself to a cup of coffee from the sideboard in the meeting room, he'd inevitably sip the drink and at the same time, unknowingly start breaking off small pieces of the Styrofoam cup as he spoke, channeling his nervousness as he got more involved in the discussion. We'd all sit waiting for the coffee to come flooding across his papers in a muddy river across the meeting table!

Life was challenging but good. After a year of sharing a house with my friend Lila, I had moved Ben and me into a townhouse in a small community north of Toronto. I needed discipline to manage my job, my responsibilities at home, and my boss at work. I learned quickly that any conversation with Gene about significant matters needed to be initiated midday, otherwise, I'd find myself caught at five o'clock in the evening, just when I needed to dash out to pick up Ben from daycare. I managed to stay healthy; this way I could care for my sick child and work from home. Then, when it was time for a vacation, my body would remind me of my vulnerability and invite all kinds of germs and illness to invade me on my own personal time. It didn't matter. I was in control of my life, and life was good.

I was developing a reputation of dependability and creativity at work. My salary was enough to support us without any child support or daycare subsidy. I focused on life with Ben rather than fighting for the pittance I would get through taking Simon to court. Even though he did not provide child support, Simon was still entitled to see Ben every other week for a daytime visit. However, he soon revealed his real focus was on himself and not on Ben. He'd show up at the daycare on his allotted day, and rather than take Ben out of the daycare to spend time with him, he would spend his precious visiting time complaining to the daycare assistants about his circumstances. Ben would sit nearby, crying and wondering why his father wasn't paying attention to him.

Attempting to take back control, Simon began to break the visitation rules after they were established by the court. He began to show up at the daycare unannounced at times during the week that were not his visitation times, demanding that he should be able to take his son out for the day. I had given the daycare the court order; they knew the rules. This was all about control. The daycare supervisor stood firm.

"Sorry Simon. Your court papers indicate you can pick up Ben every other Friday. Today is Thursday and we can't release him, so sorry!"

"That is bloody ridiculous! Ben is my son and I should be entitled to spend time with him!"

"Well you certainly are welcome to stay at the daycare and play with him if you'd like. You just can't remove him."

The daycare supervisor felt the imminent threat of this man and spoke quietly, hoping not to trigger any over-reaction. Simon quickly turned and stormed out of the daycare in a fury, muttering in his Manchester accent.

"Totally ridiculous. That bitch thinks she's in charge!"

His behavior began to become more bizarre. One Saturday, when he'd had Ben for an agreed upon full day, he called to say that we should meet downtown, so he could deliver Ben to me. I drove to the agreed upon corner of Queen and Yonge Street and waited in my car with my flashers blinking.

A pearl gray dusk was spreading across the city skyline and busy shoppers were flooding the downtown streets. Simon's taxi pulled up across the street. He parked, got out of the car, and came around to the passenger side to take Ben out of his car seat. He walked, hand in hand to the opposite corner from where I was waiting in my parked car. Once there, he released Ben's hand, patting him on the head, and quickly walked away, abandoning Ben on the corner. He almost jogged back to his car, jumped in and drove away.

I watched as our seventeen-month old was deposited and abandoned on the busy city street corner. Cars whizzed by. Streetcars clanged. Busses belched fumes. Ben began to cry, a look of total terror on his young innocent face. At any moment, he could have stepped out into the traffic. I swung open the car door in total panic, and raced across the street, yelling,

"It's Okay Ben. Just stay there. Mommy's coming!"

I ran shouting with my hands up to slow the traffic in both directions, unaware of the risk I was taking running into the street. I leapt onto the sidewalk and scooped him into my arms, my heart racing in my throat and my whole body shaking. I waited for the traffic light to turn green and returned to my car, placing him in his car seat and quietly murmuring,

"It's okay, Ben. Everything's okay. Mommy is here. Let's go home and have a snack."

It took everything I had to keep my voice calm and my hands steady on the wheel as I navigated the city streets, lights and cars streaming past me, a beehive of people bustling home from their day at work or shopping, all the while listening to my young son whimpering in the back seat. Somehow, I made it home, having driven in a trance like state, constantly assuring Ben and probably looking through the rearview mirror more than straight ahead. I was on mother autopilot.

Once the bottle and animal crackers were in his tiny hands, he calmed down, gulping and chomping happily, his face lighting up as a sign of returning security and warmth. Three days later, I found a note on the porch from Simon.

"Since I'm not even sure this kid is mine, and you are controlling the entire situation, I'm not going to worry about seeing him anymore. Good luck. Simon"

This was fine with me. There had been no child support. Now I would no longer have to deal with his harassment. I would figure out how to survive as I always had. Ben would be loved and supported without him. I couldn't worry about Ben not having a father. All I could do is try to be the best mother I could be.

Chapter Twenty-Two
The White Knight

The next six years flew by. The first year of my independence, I focused only on Ben and my work. Into the second year, I slowly began to date cautiously, but it was not easy. I was now a package deal. Love me, love my son became my new motto. There were challenging days where I'd come home and realize I'd served the role of counselor to everyone else at work in my role as Manager of Human Resources, lending my professional ear to listen to their woes, helping to solve problems, but ultimately, I was alone to deal with my own situation. There were days where I felt challenged and valued. There were other days, when I felt totally on my own and exhausted from responsibilities as a single working mother. I was out of the country, away from family. I had friends, but all were single and none had children. When my mother called, I kept my situation to myself.

"So how is everything? Do you need money? Are you ever going to settle down into another relationship or just focus on your career?"

She struggled to understand how I was managing without a man. As a war bride, she always expected her husband would be the breadwinner. It was only later in life that she found jobs to have a little 'pin money'. Now her daughter, with more education and life experiences by the time she was thirty, was forging a career path that would support herself and her child.

"You know, Mom, I told my pediatrician who asked me the same question recently: there are lots of turkeys out there to date. It only takes one to make a difference. If it happens, it happens. Meanwhile, I'm fine the way it is."

Then one warm and humid early September evening in 1985, the phone rang. It was a colleague from work named Nicole, a French Canadian who had become a good friend. She stood six inches taller than me, a willowy elegant woman with short dark hair, sporting a collection of beautiful silk scarves which she draped over her tailored suits. She smoked cigarettes through an onyx cigarette holder, giving her a movie star air. She purposefully moved from a small town outside of Montreal to Toronto, to establish a career and learn to speak English fluently. And she did. Her laughter was infectious and our friendship had grown outside of work and we would often head downtown for drinks at some of the local bars as long as I could get a babysitter. One Friday night in September, Nicole called.

"Maxene? How are you? Have you any plans for tomorrow night?"

"No not really." I never could do anything impulsively, given my parental responsibilities.

"Remember I told you about a guy I met on a Caribbean vacation who is from Toronto? I've been dating him for a while, was over at his place for a barbecue, and got to meet his older brother. Seems like a nice guy. He's divorced and has a couple of kids that he sees on a regular basis. You might have a lot in common. Can we plan to get together tomorrow night for dinner?"

"Hmm. Maybe. Depends on whether I can find a babysitter. I'll let you know."

That phone call changed the direction of my life. I got a babysitter and the next evening, I drove to Nicole's apartment, which overlooked the glow of the city's evening skyline with all its sparkle. Nicole was there with her friend, Al. After introductions, she opened a bottle of Cabernet Sauvignon and poured me a glass. Al's brother Lee showed up fifteen minutes later. He was a solidly built man in his mid-thirties with prematurely bright silver white hair, a neatly trimmed goatee and striking electric blue eyes. He wore white chinos and a black t-shirt with a sequined green and gold palm tree on the front and his name emblazoned in gold sequins on the back like a neon sign. The shirt was sleeveless. At first, I thought his sleeves were rolled up and expected to see a pack of cigarettes inside the sleeve like the stereotypical image of a long-haul trucker.

Hmmm. Attractive man. Not sure about the dress for a first date... I'll reserve judgement.

"Lee, this is my friend Maxene. Glad you could join us! Would you like a glass of Cab before we head out to the restaurant?"

Nicole seemed excited about arranging the date.

"Nice to meet you. Sure, I'll have a glass. Boy, it is hot tonight! I decided this sleeveless t-shirt was the only thing that made sense. Hope you don't mind."

186

At least he recognized his blind date dress faux pas. He does seem nice…and I love his bright white hair.

Following drinks on the terrace at Nicole's, we headed down to the waterfront to Queen's Quay to share a candlelit dinner on the restaurant patio overlooking Lake Ontario. The lights from the boats along the harbor flickered like fireflies across the water. The moon was a glowing silver disk against the blue-black sky. The air was warm velvet to the skin. Soon Nicole and Al were engaging in a heated discussion about politics. Lee and I sat quietly. I imagine both of us were trying to figure out how to extricate from the fray to enjoy each other's company. Following dinner, we headed to the harbor for a walk and some fresh air.

The next day, Lee called and asked if Ben and I would come over for dinner the following weekend. I had never had a man cook for me on a date, or even consider inviting my eight-year-old son to come along. I said 'Yes'.

The following Saturday night, we arrived at his modest home to find he had set the kitchen table with pink carnations and filled the glassware with pink cloth napkins folded like fans. He had prepared a lovely meal. I stood in the doorway taking it all in.

Is he for real? He has tried to create something wonderful. How soon will I be disappointed? I'll wait and see. Hard to believe he did this for us…

I often shared rides with a colleague from work to save gas money. One morning, about a month after I'd met Lee, we were driving to work when I started talking about my blind date, voicing my fears and concerns.

"He's very nice. I'm just waiting to see when things change. I've been through enough bad relationships. I'm a little jaded and cautious at this point in my life."

"I can understand. You've got a child and I don't blame you! He does sound nice, from everything you're telling me. Time will tell..."

Lee and I began to spend every weekend evening together, and soon after, whole weekends. I kept waiting to be disappointed and it didn't happen. Ben was eight years old, having spent the last six years without a dad. He was cautious and possessive of me. He was going to have to share me and he was not happy.

When Lee showed up at my house for the first time, Ben got out of bed and sat on the stairs, refusing to go back to bed. When I insisted, he let out a loud wail,

"No. I don't want to and you can't make me!"

I learned later that Lee was close to walking out the door, feeling he'd stepped into a situation that he couldn't influence and it might be better to exit before we got serious. Luckily, he didn't. It would take time for Ben to see the good intentions of this man without feeling it threatened his relationship with me. I had finally met someone who would be not only my lover, but my soul mate, best friend, and parent to Ben.

About four months into our relationship, we had gone for dinner at a local restaurant and were driving home. Lee started telling me about his previous marriage.

"I met my wife on a Caribbean vacation. She was sitting on the beach with her blonde haired blue-eyed little one year old boy, Craig. Truth be known, I was all of twenty-two and fell in love with her *son*. I realized the day we got married that it was a total mistake. I had married her because I wanted a family. Very naïve on my part! I even went so far as to adopt Craig, since his real dad was nowhere to be found. We were married for ten years and had two children together. Honestly, the best part about being married was being a father."

"I can tell you like it. Unfortunately, I can't say I've had much experience with a man who was interested in Ben." I gazed out the car window, realizing I had just avoided talking about my missing child by only referencing Ben. He went on to let me know his adopted son would celebrate his birthday soon.

"His birthday is coming up two days after Christmas. I'll have to think about what to get him."

The weight of his words took my breath away. I sat dumbfounded.

Can this be real? It's the same date as my daughter's birthday. Is it possible that Craig, his adopted son and my long-lost daughter have the same birthday?

Tears involuntarily began to leak down my cheeks. Lee glanced over at me and pulled the car over to the side of the road, concerned about what he might have done to make me cry.

"What's wrong? Did I say something that has upset you? Tell me what's going on?"

My story came spilling out. So many years had gone by where all I needed to do was answer certain questions without further explanation. *Do you have any children? Yes, one: a son...* I had managed to push the painful reminders of my loss deep in the dark cavern of my soul. With one simple exchange, the secret welled up like a volcano of emotion, pushing to be released.

"I can't believe it. I had a daughter when I was eighteen that I had to give up for adoption. Craig and my daughter have the same birthday." I tried to swallow hard to stop the flow of tears and took a deep breath.

"I don't know where she is and don't get to celebrate it with her, but I have celebrated in silence for the past twenty-one years."

We sat in the car by the side of the road for the next two hours, as I unlocked the door to the secret that had been buried for so long. If Lee was to know and love me, he needed to understand everything about me. Everything.

"Seriously? Unbelievable. My adopted son and your daughter have the same birthday? What are the odds?"

I slumped into the car seat and slowly nodded as the wash of sorrow welled up from deep down inside. Lee took me into his arms and held me as I sobbed.

"I know. Hard to believe. I will do my best to not wear it on my sleeve, but it's going to be very hard for me to celebrate your son's birthday. It will be a constant reminder. At least now I hope you'll understand."

This moment of truth brought Lee and I closer together. He did not judge me and simply was there for support.

The following year, we combined households and I moved into his home. One of the habits we established was to always have a room with two comfortable chairs where would we sit together after our day at work, and talk about how things had gone, and discuss our plans for the future. We had established a partnership that was new and different than anything either of us had experienced. He told me about his failed marriage to a woman who was a nurse and highly controlling. He could laugh about it now, letting me know there were only two outcomes when arguing with her:

"There was her way and the wrong way!"

Our open communication made us both stronger. It was a safe place. Here was a relationship built on trust. We often wondered when we would have our first fight. It just didn't seem to happen. Through life's tough lessons, we had both learned that when things were difficult, focus on the problem and don't attack the person. This simple rule made communication easy and constant.

Every other weekend, we were a blended family of six. His daughter and two sons would join us, and Ben and we'd spend the weekend keeping the crew active with ice skating, skiing, and Scrabble in the winter, bowling and swimming in the summer.

In the spring of 1986, a few months before the one-year anniversary of when we'd met, Lee invited me to join him at a fundraiser for a children's charity on a yacht that took partygoers around Lake Ontario. Lee represented his food service company as Vice President of Sales to corporations, and had sold the catering contract for the fundraiser to the yacht company that owned the boat. He was going to represent his company at the event. As we stood by the railing, caressed by the warm evening breeze, he turned to me.

"You know, this is a pretty spectacular way to have a party. What if we threw a party and got married on the boat?"

I leaned against the railing, feeling the gentle caress of the lake breeze, processing what I had just heard. I took a deep breath and exhaled.

"I think you just proposed to me! That sounds wonderful!"

"Okay. Let's talk to the Captain and find out if we can book it."

We entered the Captain's quarters. Lee greeted him and began the inquiry. "Hi there. Ever rent this boat for a wedding?"

"Sure have. In fact, I have an album with some photos from some of them. You interested?"

"You bet." Lee gazed over at me and smiled.

"Let me look in our log and see what's available. For this summer? A Saturday night, right?"

"Yes, while the weather is still good."

He pulled out his reservation book looking for a Saturday night.

"There's only one Saturday left this summer. It's in September. Would you like me to reserve it for you two?"

He showed us pictures of other weddings on the boat. We looked at the date and realized it was the exact date, September 6, one year earlier, when we had met for our blind date, at the restaurant overlooking the water. Lee jumped at the opportunity.

"Yes! Let's book it!"

Lee catered the event through his company. I got a brochure from the yacht company and designed invitations in blue and white featuring the boat on the front, inviting people to 'set sail'. We decided our children would be our wedding party and we would create a nautical theme. Lee, his two sons and mine all dressed alike in navy blue blazers with gold buttons and crisp white chinos and white shoes. We found a frilly white dress for his daughter; I chose a royal blue silk dress to finish off the nautical theme.

Two months later, we stepped on to the same yacht, The Jaguar Two, that the fundraiser had been on, and where he had proposed, in front of the restaurant patio where we had first met. We sailed away one year to the day onto Lake Ontario to be married in front of seventy-five friends and relatives including Lila, Toni, my parents, Lee's parents, and Ben's paternal grandparents as the sun streaked the horizon with veils of peach and gold. While our vows were taken, the Captain signaled to all the boats within range of the harbor and they blew their horns loudly, filling the air with the sound of celebration. It couldn't have been better, or so I thought.

***

Five years flew by. We worked hard, had a combined family of four children every other weekend, and grew to be a strong couple who supported each other emotionally. We moved to the country north of Toronto and renovated an older home on two acres, spending many weekends and nights doing hard labor to transform an old sixties ranch into a country place that became a magnet for friends and family.

We had blown away the back wall of the kitchen which overlooked a deck and a swimming pool and added a spacious sunroom. We painted it a creamy, happy yellow. It had a vaulted ceiling, a large palladium window with wall sconces on each side. The sunroom was filled with large potted tropical plants next to two simple wicker rocking chairs that had tropical plant-themed cushions: our special place to be at the end of our day. This was our communication place. No televisions. Just two comfortable chairs and us. We had kept a half wall between the kitchen and this room to create a bar top partially separating the two rooms. There were three bar stools snuggled up against it. A telephone sat on the bar within easy reach. We had completed the renovation and were enjoying sitting in the room one evening, sipping our Chardonnay, the ceiling fan slowly moving the air as we talked about our day. Then the phone rang.

Chapter Twenty-Three
Reunion

Lee and I were in the middle of a conversation, discussing our challenges and successes at work during the past week as we usually did. It was ten o'clock at night when the telephone rang, piercing our quiet conversation. I turned to my husband, "Who the heck would be calling at this time of night?" as I got up from my chair and answered the phone on the bar top.

"Hello? Yes." I listened to the caller intently. Lee watched, trying to figure out who it was based on half the conversation.

A husky female voice inquired:

"Is this Maxene? Hello my name is Jessie Gardner; I think I'm your daughter. I was born on December 27, 1964 in Newburgh, New York. I think my grandfather made the arrangements. I joined ALMA just two weeks ago. They are the organization that helps adoptees find their birth parents. I was always curious about my heritage and when I heard about this organization, my friend encouraged me to apply."

"Holy Shit!" Those were my first words to my daughter. It had been twenty-six years since her grandfather, the lawyer, scooped her out of my arms on the steps of the hospital. I collapsed on the bar top as she introduced herself and I muttered my expletive.

Lee sat up straight in his easy chair realizing something important was happening. I asked about what she looked like and about her adopted family and how she grew up. I tried to explain how Romolo and I were young and inexperienced and had no options.

"I understand. I can imagine it wasn't easy back then."

She assured me her life had been good, but she wanted to know where she came from and what, if any, medical history she should be aware of. I shared information about Romolo and how we had eventually married and gone to Germany and how we had ended up in Canada. She learned for the first time that she had an 'off the boat' Italian American father and a Jewish American mother.

"Wow! I can't tell you how often I've had kids in my school tell me that the way I speak and use hand gestures made them think I'm Italian even though I was raised Jewish! Unbelievable! I finally can answer that question!"

We agreed to send photographs of each other and meet the following week. She explained she lived with a roommate in Westchester, and I realized I could arrange to stay at my Cousin Joan's home, which was also in Westchester. We hung up the phone and I turned to Lee.

I could barely mouth the words. I was shaking as I told him,

"My daughter just called me! I can't believe it!"

He jumped up from his chair and surrounded me with a hug, muttering,

"This is fantastic. I'm so happy for you!"

We had been married for four years, and every year, Lee's adopted son's birthday was a bittersweet reminder for me, as we celebrated, while my daughter was out in the world somewhere. I would finally be able to celebrate her birthday for real.

***

Eight years earlier, shortly after my daughter turned eighteen, my mother had called me one evening to tell me about ALMA, the Adoptees Liberty Movement Association, an organization she had read about that helped match birth parents and adoptees.

"Maybe this is something you should consider. You realize I have refused to let your father move us from our house in Great Neck, hoping that one day she will find me and ring my doorbell. Maybe she will find you if you register. After all, she's eighteen now…"

My mother had also silently celebrated her birthday each year and lived with the guilt of having participated in this clandestine adoption. She could not easily forgive herself. However, her feelings were still mostly centered on her rather than me.

"Sure, send me the information and I'll register."

For an annual fee, you became a member; they entered your information into their database. If a match came up, they would contact the adoptee to let them know so that they could decide if they wanted the birth parent's information to make contact. It was 1982 and birth records were sealed. There was no internet, Google, laptops, cell phones, or tablets, only mainframe computers. Searching was an arduous task that required you to find a 'search buddy' and gather records from motor vehicle departments, and any other public domain where you might find information that could lead to a connection. ALMA was created in 1971 by Florence Fisher, an adoptee, who had taken twenty years to find her birth parents and had finally found her father. She decided to start this non-profit organization to facilitate others in their search.

The denial of an adult human being's right to the truth of his origin creates a scar which is imbedded in his soul forever. Alma, the Spanish word for 'soul', has a very special meaning to all adoptees, for they have been hurt in the same way*
1

Ever since I silently celebrated my daughter's eighteenth birthday, I had paid the dues to be registered. Although the organization focuses on adoptees, they also acknowledge the scar created by the loss of a child for the birth parents. I rationalized my actions.

I don't want to intrude on my daughter's life. However, if my daughter wants to find me, I want to be available. It must come from her so I know it's for the right reasons. It will probably never happen, but I can hope…

A little more than two weeks prior to that fateful phone call, Jessie was watching *The Jesse Rafael* talk show with her girlfriend Rose. One of the segments was about adoptees being reunited with birthparents through ALMA. Rose urged her on.

---

*From ALMA: Adoptee's Liberty Movement Association (http://www.almasociety.org/index.html)

"You've got to register! You've always wanted to know about your heritage and now you've got a way to do it!"

"You think this might work? It seems a little soap opera-like."

"What have you got to lose? Here, I wrote down the phone number so you can call to get the application form."

"You're right. Okay, I'll call tomorrow."

"No! Do it now!"

With her best friend's urging, Jessie gained the courage, picked up the phone and called the number. A pleasant voice answered and within minutes, they traded information and an application was in the mail for her to complete. Two days later, she filled it out and mailed it with her check to ALMA. Two weeks after she had mailed her application, she had come home from work at nine o'clock at night to find a message on her answering machine.

"Hello, my name is Carl. I have some important information for you. Please call me back as soon as you get this message." He left his phone number at the end of the message.

Jessie listened to the message and sat staring at the phone.

"I don't know anyone named Carl. It's probably a hoax." She had written his name and number on the yellow pad by the phone. She tore the note off the pad, scrunched it and tossed it in the garbage.

A half hour later, Rose called.

"Hey, how was work? Feel like coming over for a while and we'll order a pizza for our dinner?"

"Long day, but okay. Having to serve these girls who come into the shop to try on clothes and mess up my inventory and not buy anything can be so annoying! Guess what? When I got home, I had a message on my answering machine. It was some guy named Carl and the phone number was from the city, telling me he had some important information and for me to call him back. I'm thinking it's probably a prank."

"That's strange… Wait a minute! You sent an application in to a city address for the ALMA organization. You better call this guy! He might be calling from the association!"

Jessie dropped the phone, rushed to her wastepaper basket, and started digging around in the crumpled notes, telephone bills, tissues, and scratch pad doodles until she found the scrunched yellow paper missile she had tossed with Carl's phone number.

"I found it! I'm scared Rose. You think this could be about my birth parents?"

"I bet it is! You must call and find out! Call me back once you know!"

Jessie hung up from Rose and dialed the number. The same pleasant female voice answered the phone.

"Good evening, this is ALMA. How can I help you?"

"I'm returning a call from someone named Carl. Is he there?" she said hesitantly.

"Yes, who's calling?"

"This is Jessie Gardner. He left me a message earlier today to call him back."

"Just one moment please."

"Hello, this is Carl."

"Um, oh hi Carl, my name is Jessie Gardner and you left me a message earlier today?"

"Yes Jessie. Thanks for calling back. I believe we have a match to the information you provided about your birth. I have a phone number for what I believe is your birth mother's. Her name is Maxene and she lives in Toronto. She's been registered for the past eight years."

He dictated the information to Jessie. She listened and collapsed back in the chair next to the hall table where the phone sat. She wrote the number down while her head swirled in disbelief. As soon as she hung up, she called Rose back.

"I called and they are telling me they have a match to this woman who has also been registered and living in Canada. He gave me her name. What if she doesn't want to talk to me? What if she's a loser? I'm so scared!"

"I'm sure you are, but you HAVE to call her! This is so exciting and important. Just do it!"

She agreed and hung up the phone. She sat in the hallway for twenty minutes, smoothing the message paper in her hand as if to comfort herself and gain the courage, while thinking about what to say. With her best friend's encouragement, she finally took a deep breath and dialed my number.

I wasn't very poetic with my first words to her, but I guess she realized how shocked and overwhelmed I was to hear her voice.

The next day, following that fateful phone call from Jessie, I called my cousin Joan. We are only six months apart in age and had grown up like best friends, spending many vacations and school breaks together.

"Hi. I have something very important to tell you. You know I married Romolo."

"Yes, I remember Romolo."

"Well, before that, when I was seventeen, I got pregnant by Romolo and had a baby girl. We were young and we ended up giving her up for adoption. I was not allowed to talk about it. Joan, she just called me! We both registered with an organization that matches adoptees with their birth parents. Amazingly, she lives very close to you! I'm wondering if I can come to your house next weekend to finally meet her."

"Wow, of course you can! How old is she now?"

"She's twenty-six."

"Amazing. This is wonderful! I'm so happy for you; I must admit something. I have known about your situation all this time, but my mother made me swear not to reveal that I knew."

"Are you serious?"

I couldn't believe that she knew all these many years and never revealed it.

I sat dumbfounded on the phone as if I had just been told the world was square.

"You mean you actually knew what I went through all these years, but could never speak about it?"

"Yup. My mother made it clear that she would punish me severely if I ever revealed that I knew about your situation."

I sat in total disbelief of what I was hearing.

"For all these years, I have been covering my tracks and you knew all along? And now, twenty-six years later, even after your mother has passed a few years ago, you still could never open the conversation with me? How sick is that?"

"I guess I had kept it a secret for so long, it was just easier not to bring it up. Back then, we weren't allowed to talk about it and time passed. But please know I always felt your pain all these years."

Even those around me had been forced into lying, while I was working hard to cover my tracks, not realizing we were all playing this stupid dance of deception. How unreal. How sad.

The following weekend, I traveled to Joan's home to finally meet my daughter. The first and last time I had seen her, she was only four days old.

***

The doorbell of my cousin's home rang and my heart pounded with excitement and anxiety. A week before, Jessie and I had exchanged photos of each other by mail; this way we'd know how to recognize each other. It was striking to see our resemblance. Now she was standing on the other side of the front door on a Saturday evening, waiting for me to open it. Joan and her husband, Larry, were half way up their front stairs, crouching to watch the reunion and not be in the way. We stood there, staring at each other.

"Hi. Come on in. Let me get my coat," was all I could utter.

She smiled tentatively and stepped into the front foyer. My cousin's home was a large, gracious place, with a grand foyer on a wooded property in a well to do community in Westchester. Jessie's eyes wandered from the hallway to the expansive living room and back to me. I grabbed my coat and yelled up the stairs to my cousin and her husband.

"See you guys later!"

They had told me about a small Italian restaurant and I'd made a reservation for two.

Our first meeting was a turning point. We talked non-stop for over two hours while our dinners grew cold, trading stories, answering each other's questions. She asked if I knew where her biological father was and whether we could locate him. I hadn't spoken to or seen him since we divorced fifteen years earlier. We agreed that when she returned to my cousin's the next day, we would try and find him. We tentatively gave each other a brief hug, and said good night.

Joan came out of the shadows of the stairwell.

"Wow. She looks just like you." She's your height, has your cheekbones and has the same kind of voice. "Amazing! I'm so happy for you. This is incredible."

"It is surreal, Joan." My throat closed up and tears welled up in my eyes, blurring my vision. "Thank you so much for letting this happen at your house. It's such a relief to finally know her. It's going to take some time for me to get over this day."

The next day, Jessie showed up in the early afternoon and we began to search the New York phone book. We soon found Romolo's brother Ennio listed and I made the call. I launched into my request.

"Hi Ennio, it's Maxene. How are you? I'm calling you because I have something very important to tell you. I don't know if you know this, but Romolo and I had a child before we got married and we gave her up for adoption. She's found me and she'd like to meet him too. I'm wondering if you could help me to contact him?"

"Hi. Umm, yeah, Maxene, how're you doing? I'm good. Yeah, I knew about it. That's great. Let me call him and see what he wants to do. Give me your number. If he wants to make contact, he'll call you back." I hung up and we sat and waited. Ten minutes later, the phone rang.

"Hi Maxene. Is that really you? How have you been? This is unbelievable. Where are you? I live in New Jersey. Give me Joan's address. I'm getting in the car right now. I should be there in forty minutes."

I dictated the address and hung up the phone. My daughter and I sat in the kitchen sipping coffee, letting my cousin know that Romolo was on his way.

"This is so incredible. I'm so glad I could have it all happen here. Mazel Tov!"

An hour later, he arrived. His dark, wavy hair was now gone. He had only a fringe of silver gray. But his dark brown eyes still reflected the warmth of his quiet personality; the small wrinkles on the sides of his eyes told you he smiled often. His trim soccer stature remained. What an awkward wonderful moment. He hugged his daughter and hugged me. Joan took pictures of the three of us, sitting around the kitchen table, grinning. The circle was complete. Having Jessie sitting between us, there was no doubt that we had each equally contributed to her looks. Her eyes were wide and bright blue, surrounded by long lashes like mine. Her shoulder length hair was layered, rich dark chocolate, and wavy as her father's used to be. Her height was within a half inch of mine. Her fingers were tapered and fine like his. Her voice, deep like mine. Remarkable. Simply and utterly remarkable.

A few weeks later, Lee, Ben, and I traveled back to New York to meet Jessie in the city. Romolo drove from New Jersey to join us. He let me know that he had finally let his wife know about our daughter. Jessie also learned she had three other half siblings: a boy and two girls. While Romolo's wife had known he had been married before, he had decided not to talk about his 'messy past' with her and never revealed he had had a child. Like me, he had silently celebrated her birthday each December. Now, after all these years of marriage, he had to let her know he had been reunited with his long-lost daughter. I imagined it was quite a shock for her to learn this news after all this time. Like me, he probably never anticipated he'd ever meet his daughter and would have to reveal the truth.

He did not immediately reveal her real identity to his son and two daughters, who were all teenagers. It would take over a year of them meeting her numerous times and being told she was a 'friend' before he finally explained who she was. They all had a suspicion that she was related. They were thrilled to know they had another sibling.

Back at home, Jessie let her mother know she had found me. She had been told while growing up that she was adopted, however, now that she had found me, her mother's reaction was not good. She was upset to learn that her father, the lawyer who had made the adoption arrangements, had misled her as to her daughter's heritage. It was yet another reminder of his controlling nature, and she was upset to hear the news. Once again, it appeared the mother's feelings were going to supersede the daughter's.

"This is good for you. I don't need to hear any more about it. Just do what you want, and do not tell your father!"

My guess is if her adoptive father knew, he would be fine with it and potentially open to meeting me. In fact, he might have questioned why his wife was putting pressure on their daughter to keep her activities with me a secret. After all, she was a twenty-six-year-old adult, living independently. This was not something her adoptive mother could handle. Yet another secret needed to be maintained...only now it was my daughter who would need to manage it. She also told her sister and brother both of whom were adopted.

"Why are you doing this to our mother? Why is it important?" her sister asked.

"Because I wanted to know, that's why! What's wrong with that?" she responded.

"Well I don't think it's really necessary. You have a family. Be satisfied with what you've got!" was her sister's retort.

Neither her sister nor brother had any interest in finding their birth parents. I can only conjecture they were afraid of what they might find out, which is not unusual. My daughter was now going to carry the lie forward, not discussing her newfound relations with anyone in her adopted family. She would be forced to find ways to fabricate stories of newfound 'friends' that she would be visiting, rather than reveal the truth and be done with it.

Following our reunion, I needed to sit down with my thirteen-year-old son Ben, and for the first time, let him know he was not an only child. He had a half-sister whom he would no doubt meet soon. I needed to reveal where she came from and why he didn't grow up with her. I too had decided all these years that it was better and easier to not mention it unless it became a reality. And now it had. Surprisingly, he greeted the news with open excitement.

"I have a sister? Cool! When can I meet her?"

No matter where I turned, I realized we had all been a part of a conspiracy to hide the truth: whether it was my cousin to confide about my daughter, my young son, Romolo who had kept the truth from his second wife, or now, my daughter, who was being asked to hide the truth from her adoptive family. Deception was surrounding me like a heavy fog, making it hard to breathe fresh air. Was this the human condition? Is honesty such a difficult burden that lying feels better? These questions whirred in my head. What I knew was my world had only truths in it for the first time in a very long time.

Chapter Twenty-Four
Déjà Vu

In 1990, I had finally met my daughter. Each time we met, it was like lancing and healing an old wound. So much had not been expressed for so long. Not without pain. Not without laughter. Each goodbye was done through my tears, only this time they were bitter and sweet: a combination of sadness and joy, of regret and celebration.

The first year of getting to know each other presented me with a young woman who was unsure of herself, and yet had a craving to know me and my world. She slowly was unraveling her heritage and confirming she came from people who had made their way into their adulthood through trial and much error. Both her father and I had somehow managed through it all coming out the other side with a healthy family life and careers that were fulfilling. We stood as role models for what her potential could be.

After that first reunion at my cousins', I duplicated some of the pictures we had taken in her backyard and scheduled a trip to visit my parents at their winter home in Florida. I brought along Jessie's picture in a frame to present to my parents, who by now were informed of our reunion. By this time, my mother's health was taking her breath away as emphysema kept her on oxygen a great deal of the time. We all knew she could have fought the progression of her disease by exercising, but having a victim mentality, she chose to languish around the house, reading large print novels, while my father continued to ride his motorcycle to the tennis courts to join his friends and play six days a week.

I showed up at their Port Charlotte, Florida ranch with framed picture in tow. I presented it to my mother as she lay in bed one morning.

"Mom, finally, here's your granddaughter Jessie."

She took a shallow breath and simply said,

"Oh, my god...she looks like you!"

I was pleased that she had the opportunity to see her face. She never did get to meet her in person, although she spoke with her on the telephone after sending her a box of her used clothing, a strange gesture of connection that my daughter never quite understood. Why would a twenty-six-year-old want a box of used older woman's clothing? It was symbolic for my mother to do this, but the meaning was not lost on my daughter. The following year, my dad found my mother dead in her bed. I was grateful that I had closed this guilt loop before she was gone.

The reality of my mother's passing while I was living and working in Canada was a wakeup call. I couldn't imagine myself still being out of the country and receiving a phone call to learn that my dad had passed. I knew it was time to seriously try to relocate back to the United States so that I could spend my father's remaining years closer to him. I approached Lee one evening.

"Well, what do you think about moving to the U.S.? You know I always intended to go back. And now that my mother is gone, I want to spend more time with my dad."

I recall the look on his face as he smiled and responded, "Sure, let's do it!"

As an entrepreneur, he had made a significant career move into residential real estate and was doing spectacularly well. It opened a whole new challenge to our relationship as we planned our extrication from one economy into another, from our successful careers in Canada to starting over in the United States. The effort took about two years to complete and our stars seemed to align during that time. We visited Atlanta for a ReMax convention. We got to explore the city and recognized we could eliminate harsh winters, relish in a robust pre-Olympics economy in 1994, where the cost of living was much more manageable, and both transfer into Atlanta offices of our current employers. I had left *TVOntario* a few years earlier, realizing I needed American based business connections to make the employment transition that much easier. I joined a U.S. based pharmaceutical company, Baxter, as their HR manager for employee development, and got to do an assignment in Chicago for three months as an 'international assignment' out of Canada. Of course, having a U.S. passport facilitated my travel back and forth every week between the two countries.

The company was in the middle of a merger and I could see the writing on the wall if I didn't accept the assignment. Besides, this was my first foot back in the door of my home country after twenty-two years in

Canada. As anticipated, as soon as the assignment was completed, I was terminated. The experience of going through an outplacement program made it clear to me I no longer wanted to be a part of Corporate America.

I had just gone through the program and decided a good career move would be to explore consulting service companies to see if there were any opportunities. Right Associates was an up and coming global career consulting firm providing career counseling services to terminated employees. I landed a job as an account executive there, selling our services to organizations that were planning to downsize or terminate employees and wanting to ensure fewer lawsuits or bad publicity by helping the affected employees with job search training and administrative services. They had offices around the world and had recently opened an office in Toronto. Within a short time, I was exceeding budgets and deemed one of the top producers for the company in Canada.

My strategy to work for a U.S-based company so I could transition back to the States was coming to fruition. Lee and I targeted Atlanta, where there was both a ReMax and Right Associates' offices. During our next trip to Atlanta, I paid the local Right office a visit. Once they heard I had been a top producer for the Canadian operations, I was greeted warmly with a, "Hey sure; when you are ready, c'mon down. Would love to have you join our team." Lee did the same by visiting the local ReMax office. After a short visit with the broker, he received the same welcoming invitation.

In the meantime, our family grew larger, when Lee's two biological children decided they wanted to leave their mother's home and live with us. We had bought a larger house and they joined our family, leaving a note to their mother on the kitchen table one evening when she was on a late shift as a nurse, surreptitiously departing with their father. Her verbal and physical abuse over the years had taken its toll and they took a great courageous leap to do what they did in their early teenaged years, leaving their half-brother behind. It was a difficult and delicate transition with many challenges, as their mother berated them for their actions and poured guilt on them at every opportunity. Eventually, Lee's daughter, Lauren returned to her mother's, only to wind up pregnant and on her own at fifteen in 1993. This circumstance changed my perspective and uncovered much that had been buried for a very long time.

Suddenly, I was on the other side of an issue that I had carried with me for the last twenty-seven years. I was faced with being a witness to a similar scenario in a much-changed world. Now there were choices. Birth control was available if used. Abortion was possible. Welfare for 'unwed mothers' was available. My stepdaughter Lauren was presented with all her options. While her father indicated that he thought she was too young to be a mother, he let her know he would support her no matter what her decision. Her mother would have nothing of it and told her she would be on her own if she chose to keep the baby. My stepdaughter made her choice clear. She would keep the baby and figure out a way to survive.

She signed up to be on the Canadian welfare system and found a small apartment. We helped find furniture for her. Lauren gave birth to a little boy and my husband was there at his birth, while her young teenaged friends gathered in the hospital's hallways, excited about having a friend give birth. I was traveling at the time when I received the phone call about our grandson's birth. I received the news and was happy that the child was healthy, but simultaneously, the tightening of my gut reminded me that the cloud of my experience would be with me for the foreseeable future.

In 1993, we had visited Atlanta a second time for my Cousin Marlene's daughter's wedding reception. We saw a little bit more of the city and confirmed this would be our new home. By 1994, Lee and I were ready to make the move. We made one more trip to Atlanta to buy a house. His son Joel was still living with us and going to high school along with Ben. We announced our plans. Ben was ready and willing to move; having always had fond memories of times spent with my parents, especially on our Florida visits. When confronted with leaving the country to move to the U.S., Joel was conflicted. We knew this move would come with a great deal of guilt over leaving his overbearing mother and his friends. He seemed to acquiesce and we put in motion the necessary paperwork for Lee to get his Green Card, sell our home, and announce our departure from our current office and our pending arrival to our respective new offices in Dunwoody, Georgia.

In August 1994, two years before the Olympics came to Atlanta, I left Toronto first, piling Ben and our dog Buddy into my car and driving down the East Coast, visiting my brother Phil and family in Great Neck, and my college roommate Toni who was by now in Raleigh, North Carolina working for IBM. It was a wonderful trip that took about six days before we landed at my cousin Marlene's where we stayed with her and her husband, Mike, until our recently purchased home closed.

Meanwhile, Lee stayed in Canada for a few more weeks to wrap things up and then drove directly to Atlanta, closely followed by a moving truck full of our worldly possessions including Joel's things. Joel was supposed to join us later that year, but at the last minute, he backed out. We stored his boxed-up belongings and later the following year, Lee made a trip back to Canada, returning all of Joel's possessions to him. We both thought it would have been a great new beginning for Joel, but it had to be his own decision, not ours.

In 1995, his sister Lauren began to realize she was mired in a welfare world of single mothers who had learned to play the system. Things had really changed since the sixties. Having more children was a ticket to a bigger government check. Lauren began to realize this life was not what she wanted and slowly began to pick herself up. She found a job at a fast food place, so that she would have extra cash. She had had to drop out of high school and could see how limited her options were. After numerous long-distance conversations, she decided to take us up on our invitation to sponsor her and her toddler to move to our home in Atlanta.

We immediately got to work renovating our basement into a two-bedroom apartment, equipped with a small kitchen and large main area. Meanwhile, Lauren and her son, Jacob, packed up their meagre belongings and we sent her a one-way ticket to fly to Atlanta. High drama ensued when Immigration officials pulled her aside, while the plane was boarding, to inspect her paperwork. She was only eighteen with a toddler and a one-way ticket out of the country. They grilled her for answers while the plane took off without her.

Who would support her? Where would she be going? How much money did she have? What would she do when she got there? We received an emergency phone call from a tearful daughter explaining her plight. "Dad, the immigration authorities wouldn't let me get on the plane *(sniff)*. I'm stuck at the Toronto Airport, *(sniff)* and I'm not sure what to do!"

I quickly called my friend Nicole, my colleague from work who had introduced me to Lee, about the situation, asking her if she could drive to the airport and vouch for Lee's daughter, who by now was totally distraught. She had given up her apartment and was fearful that she had no place to live. Nicole raced to the airport and verified to the Immigration officials that her story was true: Nicole's friends were the father and stepmother of this young woman, and were sponsoring Lauren to move in with them in Atlanta. After a several hours at the airport, Lauren and Jacob were finally allowed to board the next plane. We greeted two exhausted travelers at the airport with much relief that night and welcomed them to their new home.

What I didn't realize until they were settled in, was what the emotional impact on me would be. I had had no counseling. I had been very good at separating my head from my heart. Here we were doing what was never done for me: providing financial and emotional support to a teenaged single mom so she could make a life for her and her son. It was déjà vu. We paid for daycare. We enrolled her in a special fast track high school so she could get her high school diploma. Every weekday, Lee got up at the crack of dawn to drive our grandson to daycare and his mom to school and did the same at the end of each school day for a year. She made tremendous progress and graduated with high grades. We were proud of her accomplishments. At the same time, Lee showered his grandson with love and attention and in my mind, became so much more than just a grandfather. He was *the* male role and father image…something I never had for Ben in his formative years.

No matter what I did to talk myself out of my deep seated emotional turmoil, I couldn't. These day-to-day interactions were a constant reminder of my own trauma. It wouldn't go away no matter what. My head told me to 'Stop it!' but my heart continued to ache. I suppose in hindsight, what was happening was that I was finally grieving for what I had missed all those years. I was seeing a young mother whose struggles were being supported by parents. She had nothing to apologize or lie about. Her life was open to the world. Mine had been hidden. The lies were constant and ever changing. The contrast was brutal and took many years to heal, more than I ever anticipated.

Joel continued to visit us each year for the next five years. Shortly, before the New Millennium, Joel announced he was finally ready to move to Atlanta. After all his visits, he realized there were many more opportunities for him in Atlanta compared to the small town in Ontario where he was hanging dry wall for a construction company. He was seeing us as the family hub with Ben, his sister and nephew, and by this time, my sister Pat from New Jersey had moved to Georgia as well. Besides, he wanted to be in the entertainment business and his future looked grim if he stayed in small town Canada.

Unfortunately, he found out that his timing stunk. He had just turned twenty-one and was an adult in the eyes of Immigration. I could no longer sponsor him as my minor stepson. He would need a student or work visa. He scurried to take his last high school course which he had (oops!) not quite finished, gain his high school diploma, applied, and was accepted into a two-year college in Atlanta, and arrived under a student visa. We greeted 2000 with Joel finally joining our family.

As the years flew by, Lee and I grew friendships and acquaintances from work and from the numerous neighborhoods we lived in. Joel and Lauren moved out on their own, as did Ben. Lee was proud and excited about my growing relationship with my daughter and his openness to include her in our family touched me. I appreciated his genuine excitement for me, but needed him to understand that the feelings were still raw; it would take practice over time to be able to speak about it openly after all these years, even after we were reunited.

This is when I began to gather my bits and pieces of writing and letters that had been hidden away along with the untold stories. I would find myself jotting down thoughts and remembrances as I traveled for business. I began to realize this was the beginning of me grabbing time and space to reflect, and begin to write my story.

Chapter Twenty-Five
Another Reunion

My college roommate Toni and I continued to have a special relationship which kept us connected through the years. We wrote while I was living in Germany, during which time she was married and divorced. We communicated when I lived in Canada and visited each other every couple of years. We talked about how it felt for me to know my daughter as an adult and she conjectured on what her daughter would be like and how she could find her. The sadness of the loss hung over her like a heavy dark rain cloud. I was the one person with whom she could express her grief, knowing I understood at a much deeper level than most.

Through all these years, neither of us truly understood the kind of underlying grief that was always there. Following her second husband's early death, she commented that at least it was clear she was grieving and the support was there to help her through it. The grief that we both endured and carried with us over the loss of our daughters, was never acknowledged nor supported. It was just something we had to silently carry with us. This was why our relationship was special; it was a safe place to express our feelings without judgement, but rather with understanding.

Toni pursued many activities including skiing, yoga, ballroom dancing, and racquetball. In 2002, while skiing, she got into a conversation with some of the guests in the lodge. They asked how many children she had and she openly commented she had three: two boys and a daughter yet to be found. The women who had asked let her know they were 'Search Angels' who volunteered to help do research for birth mothers and adopted children to create reunions. Toni jumped at the chance and gave them whatever information she had. This was now the age of the computer which facilitated these kinds of searches.

Over the next month, they stayed in touch. Then it happened. One of the women called to say she thought she had found Toni's daughter. Her name was Gabrielle and she lived north of New York City. That same evening, I received a call from Toni.

"What do I do? I have a phone number. What do I say?" She was anxious and excited.

"You make the call and let her know you believe you are her mother. The rest will just happen. I'm so excited for you. Do it when we hang up!"

It was twelve years after my reunion with Jessie that Toni reunited with her daughter. She found out her daughter was a probation officer and had been married and divorced and was addicted to pain medication after a car accident. She also drank too much. The good news was Toni also had an eight-year-old granddaughter. Their first few get-togethers were awkward, but they persisted. Toni arranged for her two sons to meet their half-sister after revealing that she existed. They were a bit shocked at the news and were slow to accept this new reality. It was easy to see this truly was Toni's daughter. The pert nose, the petite figure, the square jaw.

Gabrielle's addictions caused her to lose her job and for a while, the relationship with Toni went sideways. Eventually, she joined AA and not only straightened out, but met her future husband. It was wonderful to hear about their growing mother-daughter relationship. She could see that Toni was totally different than her parents; she thought she was a hippie. Toni explained that wasn't true. She was just a 'free thinking feminist'.

At Gabrielle's fiftieth birthday, she decided to celebrate by reuniting with the biker band that she used to sing with, and arranged a gig at a local bar. She invited Toni to celebrate with her. After all the years of secrets, Toni was finally out in public with her daughter. She was even introduced to Gabrielle's adoptive parents as simply 'a friend'. It was hard to believe they wouldn't see the striking resemblance between Toni and her daughter. She watched her sing like Janice Joplin to a crowd of friends and a well of emotion sprung from her core.

We have since talked about a mother/daughter lunch to bring her and her daughter together with me and mine. It feels right to do this, as if we are wrapping up the final chapter of a long-involved search journey.

Chapter Twenty-Six
9/11: Empty Skies

Although Simon walked out of our life in 1979, I maintained my relationship with his mother, Flo, and her second husband, Harold. They were still Ben's grandparents and there was no reason for me to forsake them. Flo told Simon directly that she was aware of his abusive behavior in his first marriage as well as with me and did not approve. Soon after this conversation, Simon wrote her off with a simple, punishing statement.

"Well if you are going to stay involved with Maxene, as far as I'm concerned, you are dead."

With that, he walked out of his mother's life, as well as his son's. *So be it*, we all thought.

Over the years, we visited Flo and Harold so that Ben knew his paternal grandparents. They attended my wedding to Lee in 1986. It was with great sensitivity that in 1994, after Harold had passed away, I had to let her know we would be leaving Canada to move to the U.S.; Flo was quite upset, but understood. By this time, she no longer heard from Simon's first wife, or saw her first grandson. We were her last relatives who had maintained a relationship with her in Canada. After we departed, I continued to stay in touch by phone, and flew back to Canada to visit with her once or twice, but

I could tell it was a very difficult time given both of her sons had abandoned her.

By 2000, at the age of eighty, her health began to fail and she moved to a nursing home, even though she still had her apartment. This is when she let me know I had been named as her executor. We had many conversations about her last wishes, including what she wanted to be buried in, and who should get her lounger chair and her small organ, her few precious things.

Then on September 11, 2001 the Twin Towers were destroyed by terrorists commandeering two planes into them, while in Pennsylvania and Washington D.C. two other planes crashed in a field and at the Pentagon. All flights in the United States were canceled. I was on the phone with my New York office when it happened. My colleagues could see the smoke billowing out of the towers south of them, and quickly excused themselves from our telephone conversation.

Two days later, on the thirteenth of September, after the terrorists had killed over three thousand people, the nursing home called to tell me Flo had died. As her executor, I now had the responsibility to settle her affairs and arrange her funeral. All flights across North America were halted. Flying there from Atlanta was out of the question. Lee, Ben, and I piled into our car within a day of that call to make the thirteen-hour trip to Toronto in one day. We stopped at a Walmart to pick up blankets so that we could take turns sleeping in the car. It was Friday. We needed to go directly to her bank to access the funds before the bank closed later on Saturday; this enabled us to have the funds necessary to pay for her funeral. We made it just in time. It was an eerie trip with a brilliant blue sky void of any air traffic and a very busy border crossing with customs officials examining every car and truck in detail to ensure there were no bombs or other terroristic items being carried.

I debited the funds and closed her account. Our next task was arranging for her funeral with the local funeral home, inviting people from her tattered address book (most of whom I did not know), ordering flowers, and lastly, buying her the pink dress in which she wished to be buried. I had no idea where Simon lived, nor was he listed in any directories; he was never notified of his mother's passing and did not attend.

Most of these tasks were done on Saturday, enabling us to have the funeral on Sunday. After driving thirteen hours straight and making the arrangements on the same day, we came back to Lee's brother's house and collapsed from exhaustion.

On Sunday, we greeted her friends and acquaintances and had the funeral. Following the service, we went to her apartment to speak with the property manager and let the residents know some of her belongings, like her television, other electronics and furniture were up for sale, while the rest would be given to Good Will.

I had honored a commitment to Flo and followed it with a brief call to one of her elderly sisters in England, letting her know of her passing. It was a sad ending of an abandoned life without any family involvement. It was the least I could do for her.

Chapter Twenty-Seven
The Secret Wedding Party 1996

I was in the middle of cooking dinner when my daughter called to tell me the news. "Daniel and I have made our plans and are getting married in March," she said, her voice filled with excitement.

At the age of thirty-two, Jessie had met the man she wanted to spend the rest of her life with. Her announcement should have led to joyous laughter, heart pounding excitement, and wedding planning. Instead, her phone call left me with a vacant place in my heart. I was not invited, nor was her father.

"Unfortunately, I can't have you there," she said, her voice trailing off. The message was bitter sweet.

Six years earlier, in 1990, I had finally reunited with her since giving her up for adoption at birth in 1964. This dark secret had permeated my life for the last thirty-two years. My daughter's birthday was the twenty-seventh of December, amidst the holiday season. For twenty-six years, the holiday season was a reminder of my loss. I would find myself moving in slow motion, unable to talk about my feelings. I would often think about her and wonder what did she look like? Was she being well cared for?

Throughout this period my parents often asked when I was coming back to the States, and all I could say is I had a great thing going in Toronto, but someday I would return. Occasionally, during phone conversations or visits home, my mother would wonder out loud about her first grandchild and express guilt over giving her up.

These were painful discussions which reminded me of my loss, and while my mother often expressed her own pain she never acknowledged mine. At least I had made it right for her; she had gotten to see a picture of her granddaughter before she died.

For the past six years, our relationship had blossomed, starting out awkwardly as we explored the parameters and potential depth of our connection. While Jessie was twenty-six when we met, in many ways, she was more like a nineteen-year-old: awkward, moody, and lacking self-confidence. As she learned of her heritage and her birth parents' successes, she began to believe she had the ability to do more with her life. I helped her with her resume and soon, she was moving into roles that gave her more responsibility in companies that could see her potential. She fast tracked from receptionist to IT Specialist, and soon was a Team Lead for a reputable company in Manhattan.

Jessie had borne the burden of fabricating stories for her parents and siblings whenever we got together, whether in Canada or New York, to honor her mother's request not to speak about anything to do with her newfound connection with me or her birth father's family. We visited twice a year as we introduced her to our children and both sides of our extended family. Over time, the same thing happened on her father's side, although it took longer to introduce his children to the fact that she was their half-sister. Overall, everyone was thrilled and accepting. Without her adoptive family's knowledge, she began to build a loving relationship with her 'other' expanding family tree, including half-sisters, half-brothers, and three step siblings as well as nephews. Her world just kept getting bigger and she kept growing because of it.

And so here we were, in 1996, talking about her pending marriage, to which her father and I were not invited. Neither of us could be seen at this momentous occasion where all her friends knew about us, as did the groom's family. Just looking at us would give away the secret: she was a mix of both parents embodied in one daughter. But we were second class citizens not to be included because of her mother's unwillingness to accept our existence.

Two weeks after her announcement, Jessie called again. "I've changed my mind. I want both of you to be there for the ceremony. But here's the deal: You need to just BE there. Don't interact with anyone or make your presence known. And unfortunately, you can't come to the reception."

I felt both insulted and elated, if that is possible. I had no choice, given the situation. I hesitated, thinking about how this would work.

"I'll call Romolo and let him know. Of course, we want to be there for you."

"If the two of you come, we'll meet you back at the hotel after the reception is over."

I was dumbfounded. After all these years of silently celebrating my daughter's birthday inside my head, wondering what she had become and whether she was happy, I was going to be able witness her marriage in person and have our own private celebration. I was excited and nervous. I told Lee who immediately talked about getting my flight arranged. I called Romolo and explained the situation.

"She changed her mind! She wants us to be there! What do you think?"

"Wow, this is incredible. Of course, I'll go. In fact, you can stay at my house and we'll go together."

I flew into New Jersey anxious about the arrangements. Romolo picked me up from the Newark Airport and greeted me warmly. I had packed a bright, turquoise, silk dress for the event. His wife was cordial and quiet, realizing this was an extraordinary occasion and she would not be a part of it. I was grateful for her respect and her willingness to support the situation.

The next day, we drove together to the Westchester Country Club where the wedding was taking place. We parked toward the back of the lot and quietly entered the Club to sit in the last row. *Once she had been mine, and I had given her away to this family in hopes they would give her a better life.* Thirty-two years later, I watched from the shadows as her adoptive parents gave her away to her new husband. I felt a raw mixture of nervous excitement, sadness, and gratitude that I was there. I managed to snap a few surreptitious pictures like an undercover agent rather than a proud parent. We were invisible, or so we thought.

Following the wedding, we left the Country Club, avoiding eye contact with the guests, and traveled to the hotel where we knew the young married couple would be staying before leaving for their honeymoon the next morning. During the wedding reception, Romolo and I sat at the hotel bar, talking about our lives and the circumstances that had brought us together again.

At ten-thirty in the evening, the happy couple showed up and found us in the bar. They were glowing and rumpled from their reception. We headed to their room and soon after, a handful of their closest friends joined us, while the bridge and groom changed into jeans and t-shirts.

"Hi. I'm Rose, Jessie's best friend," said a tall, willowy young woman with long, straw colored hair and a pleasant smile. "I was there the day she heard from ALMA and I insisted she call them back. She was nervous about doing it. I'm so glad I pushed her to make the call. It's hard to believe how much she is a blend of both of your features! Glad to finally meet!"

"I'm so grateful you insisted!" My words caught in my throat and a well of emotions stopped me from saying more.

Jessie beamed.

"I will say, you weren't exactly invisible back there wearing that shocking turquoise dress! Everyone who knew you were coming could pick you out in a flash!"

She grabbed the telephone to order three pizzas.

"I had one bite of wedding cake, but couldn't eat the whole time during the reception. I was so anxious about how we were going to pull this off and what time we'd get here! I don't know about you guys, but I'm starving!" The room filled with laughter, as we recounted the circumstances of our reunion. Romolo had been carrying a satchel with him the whole day and finally revealed its contents.

"I thought that for this special occasion, I should bring some of my homemade wine to celebrate!"

Jessie's new husband, Daniel, called the front desk for more water glasses, which arrived quickly. We poured the wine and held our glasses high in a private toast to the bride and groom. The pizzas arrived shortly after and we shared a midnight meal, spread out over the two queen beds. We took a crooked path to get here, but we were family, and together we were healing wounds and celebrating their future and ours.

Chapter Twenty-Eight
Another Perspective

It was ironic Jessie couldn't successfully conceive. Did she inherit my family's problems? After all, I hemorrhaged with both of my pregnancies, as did my mother and my sister (who had two miscarriages before finally conceiving and going full term with the help of birth control pills). We eventually all had children. Or did she just start too late? I watched depression grip her very being every time yet another friend announced their pregnancy while she just kept on trying to no avail. Everywhere she looked, she was confronted with this reality. An adoptee's desire to have someone look like them is a powerful force not to be ignored. Meanwhile, my young stepdaughter got married and produced three more children in a little more than five years.

Over those next five years, as we took our annual family vacation together, Lauren was either nursing or pregnant. It was a difficult time for my daughter to witness. I watched her jaw tense up as she tried to control her emotions seeing this young mother cooing over her latest baby or talking excitedly about her next child to come. "You'd think there is nothing else to talk about!" Jessie lamented. She was aware of how all-consuming motherhood can be. It was getting under her skin and difficult to witness. She had to learn to accept the fact it wasn't going to happen for her. It took years for her to come to terms with not conceiving. Being able to ask me and my sister questions about our medical history helped her to recognize the problem had roots in her heritage and not to blame herself. Thank goodness at least she had relatives to ask.

She refinanced their home to pay for an in-vitro procedure. She did acupuncture and herbal remedies. She became pregnant once, only to have the embryo embed in her fallopian tubes causing an emergency surgery to remove one of her ovaries. The likelihood of pregnancy was now reduced by fifty per cent and she was over forty. It was a bitter pill to swallow.

Finally, at the age of forty-four, she accepted the need to investigate adoption. She and Daniel found a lawyer couple, who had themselves adopted and based on their experience, had set up a practice to help others to privately adopt. They provided advice about the necessity to go through the State assessment, including an interview and visit to their home by a social worker. We talked about how bizarre it was that unfit parents living in terrible conditions could conceive at will and have a child without anyone inspecting, and yet a capable childless couple was to be scrutinized to qualify to care for a baby who needed a decent home. They were advised about setting up a 1-800 phone line and how to advertise in local papers to attract pregnant women who were looking to arrange for the adoption of their baby. They created a biography of themselves as potential adoptive parents that could be provided to any interested caller. And then, they waited for the phone to ring. Months went by without a call.

Eventually, several women called and after an initial conversation, never called back. It unnerved Jessie who began to feel that maybe it just wasn't meant to be. Then one evening, a call came in from a woman in her late twenties who was unemployed and had a history of using drugs. She had discovered she was pregnant from an affair with a married man. Her husband was in jail for dealing drugs. She had already had her other two children taken from her by Social Services. She was sharing a house with a male friend who encouraged her to call. She knew she couldn't care for this baby. She began to call weekly as her pregnancy continued. Jessie established a rapport with the woman, almost like a big sister. After every call, she sighed relief that they were still talking.

"I just can't wait for this to be over. She is very needy and it's draining the heck out of me."

They arranged to meet her in person at a neutral location and rented a car so that the tag couldn't be traced. They now knew what she looked like: a tall, pleasant looking woman with medium brown hair and a nervous way of speaking, as if she was expecting the world to fall apart at any moment. The weekly telephone conversations continued for the next number of months, a bittersweet connection for a mother planning to give up her child and an adopted woman who only wanted to have her own. Jessie and Daniel arranged to cover her medical costs to ensure she went to her doctor on a regular basis and that the child was healthy. They provided a lawyer for her to have her own representation.

Then the day arrived and the 1-800 number rang. The woman's friend called to say she was at the hospital and was about to give birth and have her tubes tied. The couple rushed to the hospital and called their lawyer. They called me next to express their anxious excitement. We all sat by the phone that day waiting to hear when the baby would be in her arms.

"Maxene? She's upstairs having the baby. We're waiting in the lobby hoping we'll be allowed to go upstairs soon. I'm a wreck!"

"I can only imagine. Keep us posted. We're so excited for you both! Take a deep breath. It will be okay."

There were tense moments when the mother got to hold her baby boy; moments when she almost changed her mind as the glimmer of a bond began. She cuddled him and rocked, all the while her friend was by her side, reminding her of the significant responsibility to take care of a child when she was barely taking care of herself.

"You know this is best for him and you, right?"

"Yeah I know. But look at him! He's so sweet."

Jessie and Daniel entered her hospital room, seeing the birth mother rocking. Jessie inhaled and tried to stay calm, while her insides were twisting every which way, worrying that this was not going to turn out well. Finally, the baby was handed over and she had him in her arms. They sat with the mother and her friend for a little while longer, and then finally said it was time to leave. They exited the hospital quickly, anxious that the mother might come screaming down the hallway after them. Luckily, this didn't happen. In addition, hospital rules had changed dramatically since I had Jessie and the birth mother no longer needed to exit with her baby.

They called as they were driving home.

"We've got him! I wasn't sure this was going to happen, but it has!"

I was excited for her; tears of happiness and remembered pain welled up as I recalled the day her grandfather took her from my arms. I was now living an adoptive couple's hopes, dreams, anxieties, and potential disappointments. It didn't remove my own anxiety, but gave me yet another perspective on this complex issue.

In the days that followed, we stayed in touch and could hear the excitement of two exhausted parents. Their dream was finally realized. We made plans to visit in the next month. A few days following the baby's arrival, Lee came home and handed me a small box wrapped in pink ribbon. "This is a gift for you to celebrate the arrival of your new grandson!"

I was totally surprised and slowly opened the small box to discover a tiny silver baby carriage charm with a heart on its side. I rushed upstairs to place it on my charm bracelet. He understood the significance of this huge transition in an ongoing journey of healing.

After waiting a period of ninety days, Jessie and Daniel could cancel the 1-800 number. The cord was broken and there would be no more contact with the birth mother. A Bris, the Jewish ceremony of circumcision, was performed; her adoptive family and siblings were there to celebrate.

A few weeks later, Lee and I flew up to see our new grandson. Romolo and his wife drove up from New Jersey. This would be the new pattern: her adoptive family would celebrate their grandson's birthday each year and we would either show up before or after that weekend to have our own celebration. One celebration for the two sets of adoptive grandparents and another for the two sets of birth parents and their spouses.

As Aaron grew over the next few years, a new issue came into view. What would we be called by our grandson? Who were we? He already had two sets of grandparents, and Jessie's mother didn't want to hear about me or our relationship.

"He can just call you by your name," she suggested.

I must have grimaced.

"As he gets older, he's going to want to know who we are and may talk about it to your family."

Jessie's suggestion that we just be called our birth names didn't feel right and Daniel agreed. They ruminated on it for a few more months as their son's language skills were fast developing and the time was coming to give us our names. I knew she needed to be prepared that this would happen. I was concerned that Aaron not be expected to lie or not understand who we were, just as some day he would need to be told about his own adoption. It was another instance where I was in limbo with second-class status.

Finally, on one of our annual birthday visits, we were all given our official grandparent names.

"Maxene, how about he calls you 'Nana' and Lee can be 'PopPop'? And for Romolo and Mary, the Italian names 'Nonna' and 'Nonno'," she declared.

Perfect. We felt acknowledged. We each had an identity.

Chapter Twenty-Nine
First Birthday Celebration

Starting in 2003, thirteen years after my reunion with my daughter, Lee and I began the annual tradition of a family vacation which included our children and their children. The first year, Lee surreptitiously invited my daughter and her husband to join us. They jumped at the opportunity and surprised me with their attendance. Since then we've rented houses on the beach on Jekyll Island just off the coast of Georgia twice; we stayed at Niagara-on-the-Lake in Canada; we used our own lake house in the early days before there were many off-spring; we rented a place in the Blue Ridge Mountains, and in the last number of years, have settled on Lake Lanier, Georgia as a convenient place to celebrate with a family tree that has grown to fifteen. Each of these vacations included volunteers taking on duties of organizing, shopping for food, playing games, swimming, and generally hanging out together. Jessie's specialty has been baking fruit pies that are part of the final feast on the last day of the vacation. Five days of fun without any stress. Truly enjoying each other's company.

Each year, at the end of the vacation, we wrap it up with a group photo. This group photo says it all: after five days of being together, people are smiling and relaxed, and generally looking like they don't mind still being together – a true indication that the group gets along well and enjoys each other's company. The tradition has worked so well that now we are asked way in advance for the dates in order that everyone can mark their calendars. Jessie, Daniel, and Aaron, are an integral part of these holidays. They are family.

At the five and ten-year anniversary of these vacations, we've come up with souvenirs to mark the occasion. At the fifth anniversary, we printed t-shirts with a photo of the lake house where the vacation took place; at the tenth anniversary, we had hats made with Canadian and American flags crisscrossed with our family names.

In 2014, Daniel called us to let us know he was taking Jessie and Aaron on a trip to the Caribbean to celebrate her fiftieth birthday. They had a stopover in Atlanta, and he was thinking they could visit with us for a few days before heading home. Lee and I immediately began to plan a way to have a surprise birthday party for her and invite the family. This would be the first opportunity ever for me to celebrate her birthday in person.

We ordered a special cake. I contacted her best friend Rose in New York to ask if she would like to 'knock her socks off' and attend the party with her husband and be our guests.

"Absolutely!" was her immediate response.

How fitting to have the friend that encouraged and supported my daughter to first contact me to attend this special occasion. We arranged for a videographer to document the event. I suggested that everyone consider getting her a Pandora charm to go on the bracelet I was getting her and to choose something of meaning for her. I figured this way she would have special gifts that were easy to carry home on the plane. Meanwhile, I let her know that I had arranged a manicure and pedicure as well as a massage for her birthday. This was an easy way to get her out of the house while all the decorations were arranged and guests were positioned in the house.

Following our 'Girls Day Out', we came back to the house, greasy from the massage and feeling very mellow. We walked in to the raucous noise of 'Surprise!' from our kids and their kids as well as her friend Rose and her husband from New York. Following a quick shower to wash the massage oils off, my beaming daughter reentered the living room glowing from the massage, the shower, and most importantly, the party that was waiting for her presence.

We had pulled photos from our albums of her with us at various occasions over the last twenty-four years to display. Our usual cadre of children and children's children attended. The photos reflected the many vacations and visits over the last twenty-four years spread across the dining room table commemorating her involvement with her 'other family'. A poem written by one of the guests was read to her. Tears welled up in her eyes as she declared,

"No one has ever done this for me before!"
Jessie and I both celebrated firsts that day: she finally had a surprise party and I was able to attend her birthday in person for the first time.

***

Two years later, at my surprise 70th birthday, Lee asked attendees to write me a letter to share special memories of me. My daughter's note reflected the journey and the payoff for both of us.

"Twenty-six years ago, my friend (Rose) made me register at ALMA to find you. What a great thing that was! Twenty-six years later, I have more family than I could have ever imagined. I'm very lucky to have you and the rest of the family in my life. You sacrificed a great deal to make sure I had a good life and now knowing you, it's guaranteed I will have the best, fulfilled life ever! Thank you. Love you, happy birthday! Xoxo Jessie"

These words touched me like none other. We have both gained so much from our relationship that would have been missing had we not reconnected. It is not just for the birth parent that this is important. The adopted child truly becomes a whole person if they are brought into the family and treated as a member.

Chapter Thirty
Letter Never Sent

Dear Edith:

It's been twenty-five years since I reunited with my daughter and you heard about it. I'm writing this letter to express my thanks and gratitude to you, even though I can't mail it, for raising her with love and good values.

Since I've known her, I've seen her grow from an immature girl of twenty-six into a mother with a level head and a balanced perspective about the world. I believe you and I each contributed to her fulfillment in different ways. You gave her a foundation. I gave her roots and a belief in her inherited genetic capabilities. We should both be proud.

And yet, we have never met and you refuse to acknowledge me or my contribution. Why? You are in your late seventies and *still* suffer from a neurosis about your lawyer father who apparently betrayed you? After all these years, and with him long gone, can you not forgive and focus on the road ahead of you and your daughter? Can you not see how she has become more fulfilled by finding out about her roots, her heritage? There is nothing about it to be ashamed of. In fact, I believe you would find an even richer closeness if we met and you could appreciate just a little of the suffering I endured that enabled you to be her parent.

Can you not step out of your shoes and into mine for a moment? Or better yet, step into your daughter's shoes to experience her delight at finding her two extended families? Are you not happy for her rather than threatened by it? What is being taken from you? Nothing.

Ask yourself: What would it take away from your life? What would it add? In your twilight years, you could be opening yourself up to so much more. But instead, I'm afraid your world is shrinking.

You never would allow her to tell your husband of my existence in her life. What were you keeping from him? The potential that he would have been happy for her and accepting of me? What a shame that he died never knowing. It was a missed opportunity to celebrate your daughter's discovery rather than hiding it from him because it somehow threatened you.

Even her in-laws have been afraid to meet me over the last twenty-five years; for fear that a slip of the tongue when they were with you might reveal something by mistake. What an unfortunate situation. Lies, lies, and more lies continue to surround me! Is this the inevitable human condition? At last, this weekend, while visiting 'our daughter', her in-laws finally asked for us all to visit. Then a wicked blizzard blew into the northeast, blanketing the roads, making it hazardous to travel. We spent the weekend playing games, eating, and drinking wine, gazing out the window at the crystalline blanket covering trees, bird feeders and cars. I truly hope there is another opportunity to meet them and validate my existence.

Something you still and probably always will deny. I will always be a hidden part of 'our daughter's' life. So, the lying from the past twenty-five years continues. She will never be free to openly express her happiness or sadness about our relationship, even though you have known her far longer than I have. You deny her the right to express who she truly is today. You are missing a major piece of her experience as a mature woman, while I, ironically, have no lies between us and hear about her *whole life* as it unfolds today. It saddens me.

Ultimately, your world is getting smaller by the day, while mine continues to expand. I'm truly sorry that you couldn't invite me into your world so that we could each say 'Thank You' in person. You and I both deserve it.

Sincerely,
Our Daughter's Other Mother

Chapter Thirty-One
Telling the World

Occasionally, Lee would come home to announce that he'd just worked with a nice couple whom he helped to buy a house and now he thought it would be appropriate to thank them by inviting them over for a celebratory dinner. He and I would plan our menu and share responsibilities to put on a spread. There would be appetizers, good wine, and some of his great Caesar salad followed by a grilled main course. I would bake a treat to finish off the evening's repast. Our conversation would begin by sharing the couple's play by play excitement and stress of purchasing or selling their home and would soon wander toward more personal stories about travel, heritage, and family.

When asked how many children there were in our blended family, Lee would chime in that we had five grown children between us: he had three and I had two. Then he'd proceed to launch into my story, revealing how my daughter was given up for adoption at birth and how we reunited. I would find myself shrinking under the dining room table, tense jaw, heart racing as he openly and with pleasure, revealed my secret.

"Yes, and now she's a part of our family and we see her often including at our annual a family vacation." He beamed telling the story.

I just never knew how people would react and was not used to this kind of open revelation to almost strangers.

I had just met these people. I had spent my whole adult life protecting the secret as if it was an infectious disease that should not be shared. It didn't matter that we had reunited. My secrecy muscles were still in play. Every time he told my story, it was like opening the door to a dark cave and lighting a candle, letting strangers peer into its depths, not knowing their reaction. Assuming their acceptance.

As they asked me questions, my throat would close and I would find myself fighting old tears as I tried to answer their questions, working hard to control my emotions and discomfort.

Uncomfortable and yet relieving. A pain that required careful treatment, going around the edges, trying not to strike at its center. And yet once struck at its center, the pressure of concealment would begin to subside.

Later in the evening, after our guests had left and we were cleaning up, I tried to explain my discomfort. "You know I'm not comfortable having you tell strangers about my situation. I've only selectively told people I know well. After all, it's MY STORY. I'd like to be the one to determine who we tell." I was emotional as I tried to explain my feelings.

After all this time, why was I reacting this way? Jessie and I had reconnected. It was no longer a secret, right? And yet, it was and is. Even today, there are tons of colleagues at work who do not know. Why should they? Would it distract or taint my image or their understanding of me? Maybe. Maybe not. It has always felt like it needed to be compartmentalized: the automatic need to separate head and heart that I had practiced for all these many years – not for professional consumption.

Lee's excitement about our daughter – and that's how he has felt about her ever since our reunion – has slowly helped me to get comfortable with revealing my story. I guess after telling it more frequently over the years, and seeing the positive and empathetic reaction of so many, it has helped me to realize it's a story to be shared. Thus, this memoir.

As I've written and researched the subject, it has become therapeutic. I'm seeing a pattern of behavior as a direct reaction to giving up my daughter that I now know is not unique to me. The dark secret ruled my inner emotions, whether I acknowledged it or not. I've read books like *The Girls Who Went Away* by Anne Fessler, and discovered one hundred other stories of women who felt they had no choice but to give their child up for adoption. I've begun to recognize the buried conflict within me: a feeling of failure and yet a strong will to be successful. I've come to terms with how I punished myself by getting involved in an abusive relationship and yet desperately wanting to be a mother to my own child, even if I was under the worst of oppressive conditions.

It is strange to reflect on the fact that my college roommate Toni did the same thing by marrying an abusive husband and having a child with him. The human spirit thrives despite bad decisions; the will to thrive continues against all odds.

Chapter Thirty-Two
Into Her World

I had business reasons for being in New York and contacted Jessie to see if we could meet up for lunch before I headed back to the airport and traveled back to Atlanta. I showed up in my business attire, having just ended a tough meeting with a prospective client.

"Love your outfit! Let me give you a tour of our offices."

She wore black slacks and a flowing black and gray blouse that accented her dark hair and bright blue eyes. No sooner did we leave my suitcase and briefcase by her cubicle, then it began.

"This is Maxene!" Jessie smiled as she addressed colleagues in cubicles all over the office. They immediately popped their heads up over their cubicle walls, like eager gophers, eyes wide as they stared at me with mouths chattering as they openly declared their amazement at our similarities.

"She's even your height and her gestures are the same! Now I see where you get your deep voice from!"

Validation. The feeling of connectedness to someone who has always been there in your world, but not visibly a part of their life. Pride in knowing that you're finally accepted and acceptable to show to a part of her world.

For so many years The Situation, The Dark Secret existed. Finally, finally, like a broken dam whose waters come rushing out to find their natural level: the truth had been spoken. Out loud. In public. The journey had gone from Good, to Better. With my acknowledgement in her world, it became Best. I held back the tears that wanted to force their way out into public view. The grin on my face was so wide it began to hurt. A good hurt. I took a deep breath and realized that all of this was good. And it felt all right.

Biography of Maxene Raices

Maxene Raices completed her Masters of Education at the University of Toronto, Ontario Institute for Studies in Education, as well as a B.A. in English from New York State University at New Paltz. Her experience includes English teacher, Manager of Human Resources, and Senior Account Executive for three consulting firms developing business in the career management and training services industries. She is an active member of the Atlanta Writers Club. Maxene writes about her observations of life on her blog which can be accessed at *maxene-raices.com*. Additionally, she has written and presented in numerous professional human resources venues and is comfortable doing both.

She lives in Alpharetta, Georgia with her husband, Lee. Her son as well as Lee's daughter and son also live in Georgia. Her daughter still lives in New York with her husband and son and has been an integral part of the family for the past twenty-seven years.